How [illegible]n Make Full Proof of Your Ministry

Dag Heward-Mills

Parchment House

Unless otherwise stated, all Scripture quotations are taken from the King James Version of the Bible.

How You Can Make Full Proof of Your Ministry

First published 2017 by Parchment House
2nd Printing 2018

Find out more about Dag Heward-Mills at:

"Healing Jesus Campaign
Email: evangelist@daghewardmills.org
Website: www.daghewardmills.org
Facebook: Dag Heward-Mills
Twitter: @EvangelistDag

ISBN : 978-1-68398-194-7

Contents

CHAPTER 1

Divine Events That Make Full Proof of Your Ministry

But watch thou in all things, endure afflictions, do the work of an evangelist, MAKE FULL PROOF of thy ministry.

2 Timothy 4:5

It is possible to make full proof of your ministry. The ministry of Jesus Christ is the most important activity you can ever be involved in. The greatest privilege given to a human being is to work for God. Working for God is called 'ministry'. It is of utmost importance that you make full proof of your ministry. It is of utmost importance that you complete any assignment the Lord gives you on this earth. Do not die without making full proof of your ministry.

You will not enjoy your arrival in heaven if you have not fulfilled your ministry.

You know what it is like to do an exam that you are not prepared for! You know what it is like when your supervisor finds you unprepared and unready with your work.

> **And say to Archippus, Take heed to the ministry which thou hast received in the Lord, that thou fulfil it.**
>
> **Colossians 4:17**

Most people would say that they do not know what their calling is, let alone know how to fulfil it! How much more knowing how to make full proof of their ministry! This book is about how to fulfil your ministry. If you are reading this book, you do have a ministry. Notice the strong warning that Paul gave to Archippus, "Fulfil your ministry". In other words, make sure you fulfil and complete your ministry.

Many people say, "I do not have a gift like you do and I do not have a spiritual office." The truth is that most of us do not feel specially gifted in ministry. In reality, many have been separated by God but do not respond to it. Many people have been shown love but do not respond to it.

If you think you are going to see an angel before you respond to the call of God, you are likely never to respond.

To make full proof of your ministry, you must understand how God calls you and directs you into fruitfulness. To fulfil your ministry, you must respond to the divine events of your life.

Divine Events

Most people do not understand what divinely orchestrated events are. Whether you understand or not, failure to respond to the divine events of your life will guarantee that you will not fulfil your ministry. Most people do not fulfil their ministries because they do not respond to the divinely orchestrated events of their lives. What are these divine events? The divine events of your life are:

1. The divine drawing. (John 6:44)
2. The divine desires. (1 Timothy 3:1)
3. The divine convictions. (John 16:7-8)
4. The divine love. (Deuteronomy 6:5)
5. The divine mercy of God. (2 Corinthians 4:1)
6. The divine separation. (Deuteronomy 10:8)
7. The divine will of God. (Ephesians 1:9)
8. The divine calling. (Romans 1:1)
9. The divine mission. (Jonah 1:1-3)
10. The divine purposes. (Proverbs 16:4)
11. The divine visions. (Acts 26:19)
12. The divine impartation of gifts. (Romans 1:11)
13. The divine grace. (2 Timothy 1:8-9)
14. The divine office. (Romans 12:4)

There is no use pretending that you need to hear a literal voice before you know what to do with your ministry. There is no use claiming that you are waiting for Jesus to appear to you before you know what you are supposed to do. There are many divine events that will guide you towards your real ministry and help you to fulfil it.

The mysterious will of God, the purpose of God and God showing you mercy are powerful life-changing events that will lead you directly into the ministry.

Without responding to the mercy and the love of God, you will never be in ministry. Paul said that he was constrained by the love of God. Your separation from your family, your country and your people is an important spiritual event that has taken place in your life. Responding properly to these spiritual events will make you fulfil your ministry.

CHAPTER 2

Follow the One You Are Drawn To

No man can come to me, except the Father which hath sent me DRAW HIM: and I will raise him up at the last day.

John 6:44

Follow the person you are drawn to and you will make full proof of your ministry! Being drawn to someone is supernatural. Have the fear of God in you and have a proper respect for whom God is drawing you to. As you follow the people you are drawn to, you will make full proof of your ministry!

1. If you are being drawn to God, you are having a supernatural experience.

Being drawn to God is supernatural. It is the Father who is drawing you. Many people do not like God! Many people do not want to pray or fast. Many people do not like the Bible! Many people do not like church. To be drawn to something is to be attracted to it. God puts it in your heart to be attracted to Him and to the church!

You may find yourself being drawn to church, to Christian things and to God. It is so subtle that you do not even notice that you are gravitating towards the church and not the nightclub.

It is important to recognize what you are drawn to. All of us are drawn to different things. When you recognize what you are drawn to, you will begin to recognize your calling and you can start to fulfil your ministry.

2. If you are drawn to a man, you are also having a spiritual experience.

What is the difference between being drawn to someone and desiring something? When you are drawn to someone, you find yourself gravitating towards the person. You find yourself being interested in what the person says and does. When you desire something, there is a stronger internal yearning for that thing. A desire creates a stronger impression on you than a "drawing".

3. It may be difficult to recognize when you are being drawn.

To recognize what you are drawn to is probably the most difficult spiritual experience of all. This is because when you are being drawn to God, you do not notice what is happening to you. You just keep finding yourself in the church, in a fellowship, at a meeting and with the brethren.

4. You will be drawn to the men of God that the Father chooses.

No man can come to me, except the Father which hath sent me DRAW HIM: and I will raise him up at the last day.

John 6:44

You may be drawn to a man of God! God will draw you to the men He wants you to learn from. Most men of God are liked by some and despised by others. The same man of God who enchants you may irritate other people.

You may be captivated by a man of God, while someone else cannot stand the same person. No one can come to God unless the Father draws him. It is often the Father who draws you in a very subtle, unnoticeable way to Himself through His servant. Jesus pointed out clearly that no one would be attracted to Him unless God worked on the person's heart and drew him. Jesus was not liked or loved by every one. The majority of the Jews called for His crucifixion. Not everyone thought He was a great guy. Jesus explained this phenomenon to us when He said, "No one can come to me unless the Father is drawing him." Jesus recognized every single person who was drawn to Him because He knew that it was supernatural for someone to be drawn to Him.

5. **You will be drawn to different people at different times.**

> **Again the next day after John stood, and two of his disciples; and looking upon Jesus as he walked, he saith, behold the Lamb of God!**
>
> **And the two disciples heard him speak, and they followed Jesus.**
>
> **John 1:35-37**

Throughout your ministry, God will place in you an inexplicable attraction to the people that are important to the fulfilling of your ministry. It is important to recognize the supernatural drawing of the Holy Spirit. Accept that the Holy Spirit is drawing you to certain people.

Even John's disciples were drawn to Jesus when they heard of Him. They left their master, John the Baptist, and followed Jesus Christ from the day they came into contact with Him. John the Baptist was comfortable with that because he knew that he was just a forerunner to introduce Jesus to the world.

Throughout my ministry, I have noticed a drawing and an interest in different men of God. These people have been very important to the fulfilling of my ministry. They have complimented one another in the roles they played in my life. I was drawn to Kenneth Hagin as a teenager. I am still drawn to him even though I am in my fifties. I have also been drawn to other men of God at different seasons of my life. These men have had a great impact on my ministry.

CHAPTER 3

Accept Rejection and Fulfil Your Ministry

He came unto his own, and his own RECEIVED HIM NOT. But as many as received him, to them gave he power to become the sons of God, even to them that believe on his name:

John 1:11-12

1. Most ministers are rejected before they are accepted.

Rejection is a necessary season that you have to endure in ministry. John Wesley was rejected by the Anglican Church and forced to preach outside the established churches. Some of his famous sermons were delivered in cemeteries. He once stood on his father's tomb and preached a powerful message. However at the end of his life, when he was in his seventies and eighties, all the pulpits that had been closed to him were later open and welcoming to him.

Hardly is there anyone who is accepted without an initial rejection. What is important is that you are accepted by God.

2. Moses was rejected by the Israelites.

They rejected him as their leader. "Who do you think you are?" was the response they gave to Moses when he tried to save them. It was only after this rejection that he went into the wilderness to find God for himself. It was when he had found God, that he was finally accepted as the leader of the Israelites.

> **And he said, Who made thee a prince and a judge over us? intendest thou to kill me, as thou killedst the Egyptian? And Moses feared, and said, Surely this thing is known.**
>
> **Exodus 2:14**

3. Jesus was rejected by the Israelites.

Most of the Jews rejected Jesus. He came to His own and His own received Him not. Jesus has been rejected as the King of the Jews. It is only when He comes in glory that He will be accepted by His own people.

Today Christianity is a religion of the Gentiles. The Jewish nation and the Jewish people absolutely and totally reject Christianity.

> **He came unto his own, and his own received him not.**
>
> **John 1:11**

4. Rejection occurs at the same time as you are being drawn to someone.

Many times, being drawn to God happens simultaneously with your being rejected by the world. Do not be sad that you have been rejected by the world. In the midst of your rejection, you start gravitating towards God's divine appointment for you.

I found the Lord when I was in secondary school. I was drawn to God at the same time as I was rejected by many of my schoolmates and friends. Because I was half-caste, brown coloured, a person of mixed race, I was rejected and considered a foreigner and even a white man. My rejection consisted of extra punishment, bullying and continuous mockery.

I dearly wanted to be accepted and befriended. Every young person wants to be part of the crowd. One day, an older half-caste student quietly explained what was happening to me. He said I was experiencing a lot of suffering, unfair punishment, bullying and wickedness because I was half-caste. He advised me to focus on my studies and keep to myself in the boarding school.

I began to understand that I was different and I simply was not accepted as a normal Ghanaian boy. It was about that time that I met a group of born-again Christians. They were an amazing group of Ghanaian brothers and sisters. I felt so much acceptance and love. Without realizing it, I was drawn to them and kept yearning for their company. They gradually became my best and only friends in the hard and wicked school environment. God had used my rejection to draw me to Himself and to His people.

5. Rejection is painful but necessary for your purification.

> **Now when Pharaoh heard this thing, he sought to slay Moses. But Moses fled from the face of Pharaoh, and dwelt in the land of Midian: and he sat down by a well.**
>
> **Exodus 2:15**

Rejection results in isolation. Isolation ensures that you hear from God and God alone.

Rejection is important because it prevents you from following the crowd.

Rejection ensures that your ministry does not follow the mistakes of the others ahead of you. Because you have been rejected, you are forced to learn from God directly.

Rejection ensures that the pattern of God for your life and ministry is not contaminated.

6. Rejection is an important form of guidance for your ministry.

And the Lord said unto Moses, When thou goest to return into Egypt, see that thou do all those wonders before Pharaoh, which I have put in thine hand: but I WILL HARDEN HIS HEART, that he shall not let the people go.

Exodus 4:21

And the Lord said unto Moses, See, I have made thee a god to Pharaoh: and Aaron thy brother shall be thy prophet. Thou shalt speak all that I command thee: and Aaron thy brother shall speak unto Pharaoh, that he send the children of Israel out of his land. And I WILL HARDEN PHARAOH'S HEART, AND MULTIPLY MY SIGNS AND MY WONDERS in the land of Egypt.

Exodus 7:1-3

Rejection represents a closed door. Once you are rejected, you cannot go forward. You cannot preach to those who do not want you. You cannot speak to those who don't like you. You cannot travel to places where your message is not welcome. You cannot have meetings with those who don't like your style. However, you will discover people who simply adore you and enjoy everything about you. That is the field carved out for you. That is how to identify your harvest fields. Consider your rejection as a divinely shut door. God sent Moses to Pharaoh. Pharaoh's heart was hardened. It is the hardening of Pharaoh's heart and the rejection of Moses that led to the mighty miracle ministry of Moses. Moses is famous for signs and wonders. But those signs and wonders would not have been possible if Pharaoh's heart had not been hardened by God. Even as God was sending Moses to Pharaoh, He told him that He would harden Pharaoh's heart. In others words, God wanted Pharaoh to say 'NO' to Moses. Indeed, rejection is a form of spiritual guidance! You must learn to follow what the rejection is leading you into.

I once wanted to borrow money from a bank to build a church. Thankfully, the banks refused to give me any help. When I was rejected by the banks, I was forced to learn how to live without loans and debts. That was a divine form of guidance for me into a life of debt-free prosperity. Learn to recognize what God is guiding you into, (or away from) by the experiences of rejection you have.

7. Jesus was rejected in Nazareth but accepted in Galilee.

Jesus could not do miracles in Nazareth. In Galilee he did many mighty miracles whereas in Nazareth, they attempted to throw him off a cliff. They wanted him dead because they accepted him as a carpenter but rejected him as a prophet. They just couldn't accept that a well-known carpenter had turned into a man of God. Jesus Christ, accepting the rejection from Nazareth, moved quickly to Galilee where he was well accepted.

It's time for you to move on quickly to the people and places where you will fulfill your ministry in a great way.

CHAPTER 4

Follow Your Desires

This is a true saying, IF A MAN DESIRE the office of a bishop, he desireth a good work.

1 Timothy 3:1

Follow your desires and you will make full proof of your ministry! Desiring someone and desiring something are more supernatural than you imagine. Have the fear of God in you and have a proper respect for your desires. As you follow your desires, you will make full proof of your ministry!

1. A spiritual person must pay attention to his desires.

It is very important to pay attention to your desires. Your desires are used by God to do His will. As far back as the Garden of Eden God decided to use desires to accomplish His will.

2. God places desires in men to accomplish His will.

In order to re-populate the earth, God placed a desire in women for men. This inexorable and inexplicable desire is now within every woman and is working out God's purpose of replenishing the earth.

> **Unto the woman he said, I will greatly multiply thy sorrow and thy conception; in sorrow thou shalt bring forth children; and THY DESIRE shall be to thy husband, and he shall rule over thee.**
>
> **Genesis 3:16**

Even though women have no good reason to desire men who oppress them, they are constantly filled with a yearning and a longing for men. Today, many women are more open about their need and desire for a husband. One lady said, "I'd rather die than not be married." Desires have been used from ancient times to accomplish the will of God and today; God is still using desires to accomplish His will. God uses your desire to accomplish His will. Watch out for your desires! They are divine instruments in the hands of God.

3. The desire for things disappear when the mission is over.

The end of desire is usually the end of the mission. Desires do genuinely fail and stop completely. A person who is at the end of his life's mission is usually without a desire to live. A person at the end of his life's mission has no desire to accomplish anything new.

It is a very sad thing when there is no more desire! The failure of desire is like heart failure, kidney failure or liver failure in the sense that a major organ has stopped working. Desire failure (a lack of desire) is as devastating as heart failure or kidney failure. A lack of desire completely changes a person. A lack of desire causes a person to behave abnormally and function way below his purpose. A lack of desire is usually found in people near death.

> **Also when they shall be afraid of that which is high, and fears shall be in the way, and the almond tree shall flourish, and the grasshopper shall be a burden, and DESIRE SHALL FAIL: because man goeth to his long home, and the mourners go about the streets:**
>
> **Ecclesiastes 12:5**

4. There are many evil desires, but there are also good desires.

Most people are afraid of their desires. This is because human beings often have desires for wrong and illegal things. Men have desires for women, pornography, masturbation, sex and homosexuality. You cannot blame a man for being wary of his desires. However, the more spiritual you become, the more you realise that not all your desires are evil.

5. The call of God is usually accompanied by a desire.

When God calls you, he often places a desire within you. You will notice your strong and passionate interest in certain things. Your love for God, your love for soul-winning, your love for church, your love for God's house will be all that fires you up. This desire is a sign that you are called by God. Always look out for desires. Desires are very important navigators for Christians who are seeking God's will in life. This is why Paul said to Timothy, "Watch out for those who have desires."

This is a true saying, if A MAN DESIRE the office of a bishop, he desireth a good work.

1 Timothy 3:1

Paul asked Timothy to look out for those people who had desires to be bishops. Remember that very few people have such desires. Very few people desire to be pastors and ministers of the gospel. Such desires are divinely imparted. I have learnt to respect people's desires for the work of God.

Sometimes God places in you a desire for loving and serving Him. God places in you a desire for soul winning and church planting. These "unnatural" desires are implanted in you by Almighty God.

6. God can place in you a desire for an entire nation.

He can put in you a desire for a nation or a group of people. Paul had a strong desire for the salvation of his relatives, the Jews. There are times I have felt a strong desire for the salvation of certain nations. I have found myself weeping and praying for their salvation.

Brethren, my heart's desire and prayer to God for Israel is, that they might be saved.

Romans 10:1

CHAPTER 5

Follow Your Convictions

But I tell you the truth, it is to your advantage that I go away; for if I do not go away, THE HELPER will not come to you; but if I go, I will send Him to you.
And He, when He comes, will CONVICT the world concerning sin and righteousness and judgment;

John 16:7-8 (NASB)

Follow your convictions and you will make full proof of your ministry! Following your convictions is following the supernatural. Have the fear of God in you and have a proper respect for your convictions. As you follow your convictions, you will make full proof of your ministry!

What You Must Know About Convictions

1. It is the work of the Holy Spirit to make you have strong convictions.

A conviction is a strong belief about something. One of the main works of the Holy Spirit is to give convictions. Notice that when the Holy Spirit comes He will convict the world of various things. The work of the Holy Spirit is to convict human beings. The Holy Spirit gives you strong beliefs, strong attitudes and strong opinions about certain things.

When I was in secondary school I had a strong conviction to serve the Lord. I believed that I was called by God and that I had to work for Him. This conviction was in me as I walked to the examination hall to take my 'A' Level examinations. I remember walking down the road towards the examination hall and thinking about how I was going to serve the Lord. I did not even know what it meant to serve the Lord, but a strong conviction was forming in me.

2. No one can tell how the convictions from the Holy Spirit are formed.

Sometimes you cannot tell how these strong opinions are formed. For seven years I was in medical school studying all kinds of subjects: anatomy, physiology, surgery, pathology and so on. After seven years, my conviction to be a minister of the gospel was even stronger. Nothing I learnt in the medical school changed my mind. I was thoroughly convinced that I had to work for God and win souls for him. How did such a strong conviction come to me? It must have been the Holy Spirit! I had no idea I would be a pastor of a big church. I could not have imagined what the ministry would be like today. I did not even know anyone who was a medical doctor and left his profession for the ministry. I did not know any pastors, whom I could relate with. I just had a conviction and I needed to serve God badly.

3. The strongest convictions are life and death convictions.

Apostle Paul had a strong conviction about his calling too. He said he would die if he did not preach the gospel. That is strong! When you believe something to the point of life or death, it is a strong conviction. A young man came to me one day and said he wanted to be in ministry. I asked him to go and get a secular job for some time. He told me that he would obey me but felt he would die if he did not go into the ministry. At that point, I knew that the Holy Spirit was calling him and giving him the strongest kind of conviction. I decided to help him come into full-time ministry because of the strong life and death conviction that he had.

4. Look out for whether people have a real conviction about the ministry.

This is what I look for when I interview people about the ministry. I want to see whether they are really called and whether they have a conviction to serve the Lord or not. You need to have a strong conviction before you come into the ministry. You must not come into the ministry to get a good salary or a good car. Those things may be provided, but the real foundation for entering into full time ministry is a conviction.

5. You can walk away from a job but you cannot walk away from a conviction.

One day, a pastor handed in his resignation letter and quit ministry suddenly. He said he was going to pursue a secular career in another nation. I was shocked! Why was I shocked? I was shocked because the basis for coming into ministry is a conviction from the Holy Spirit about what you must do. If you had such a strong conviction, why do you suddenly resign and walk away without even a five-minute discussion? Is it so easy to walk away from a conviction?

It is easy to walk away from a job! It is easy to walk away from a secular school, but you cannot walk away from your conviction. Your conviction stays with you even when you are far away in the stomach of a whale.

Remember that Jonah could not get away from his conviction to serve the Lord. Even in the belly of the whale he knew he was to blame for his own calamity. Convictions are not easy to dispense with. Someone asked me, "How do you stay on course? How come you still have the same zeal that you had many years ago?" I am often amazed about that question because I do not do anything to keep the fire. I am simply following the conviction I have had since I was a child. I am doing what I strongly believe in.

6. Follow your convictions earnestly.

Do you have any convictions? Make sure you follow them. Strong unshakeable beliefs are divinely imparted by the Holy Spirit! I followed my convictions earnestly and it brought me into a large ministry which I could not have known about. God knows about many things but He does not tell us with English words. He tells us very little but gives us convictions about what we have to do.

Make sure you follow your convictions because your convictions will not go away. The strong beliefs you have were not formed by chance. They were formed by the Holy Spirit working in you.

CHAPTER 6

Respond to the Love of God

And THOU SHALT LOVE THE LORD THY GOD with all thine heart, and with all thy soul, and with all thy might.

Deuteronomy 6:5

Respond to the love of God and you will make full proof of your ministry! Responding to the love of God is to follow something supernatural. Have a proper respect for the love that God has shown you. As you respond to the love of God, you will definitely make full proof of your ministry!

Simply loving God will be a great guide for what you have to do in ministry. God showing you mercy is a divine and mysterious event that you are expected to respond to. Most Christians and ministers take the mercy of God for granted. This is unfortunate. Failing to see God's mercy and grace at work in your life is to fail to see God's expectation of you. It is because God loves you that He has shown you mercy and allowed you to escape certain things. You must see the love that God shows to you and interpret it appropriately. You must know and understand the love that God has for you.

> **And we have known and believed the love that God hath to us. God is love; and he that dwelleth in love dwelleth in God, and God in him.**
>
> **1 John 4:16**

When the apostle Paul was shown mercy and love by Jesus, whom he was persecuting, he interpreted it rightly. Paul responded to the love that was shown to him! God's love and mercy to Paul was a divine event that led him into his ministry. Indeed, Paul constantly referred to this mercy when he spoke about his ministry. You can only fulfil your ministry when you understand the deep mercy that has been shown to you.

If God has shown you much love, your response to that love is to love Him back with an equally strong and sincere love. If you respond in the right way, you will fulfil your ministry.

Love and the Ministry

Ministry is done out of love! Love makes you do certain things. Responding to this great mercy is the way to start your ministry and to fulfil it! A large part of your ministry will take place if you respond to the divine event of God showing you love.

Love is a powerful guiding force that will lead you on the road to true ministry. Love leads to particular works. Notice the scripture below. You will notice that, 'your first love is linked to your first works.' In other words, a certain kind of love leads to a certain kind of fruit.

> **Nevertheless I have somewhat against thee, because thou hast left thy FIRST LOVE. Remember therefore from whence thou art fallen, and repent, and do the FIRST WORKS; or else I will come unto thee quickly, and will remove thy candlestick out of his place, except thou repent.**
>
> **Revelation 2:4-5**

This is the strong message that the Lord had for His church. ***You have fallen from your first love and first works. I want the first love back with its attendant first works.*** It is your love for God that determines the work you can do for Him. Ministry is not a secular job. There is no amount of money that can motivate you to truly love and minister to people. God the Father was motivated by love for the people. God gave His only Son to die on the cross for us because of love. Jesus Christ Himself was motivated by His love for us. Jesus was motivated by greater love. 'Greater love hath no man than this, that a man lay down his life for his friends.' (John 15:13). When you have love, you do not need to be given details of what you must do.

You must respond to God's love with an equally high quality of love. The only appropriate kind of love that will make you fulfil your ministry is the kind the Bible calls first love. You must work for God with first love. When you work for God with first love you will do the right kind of works.

Indeed, anyone who works for God without love will do the wrong things for the wrong reasons. First love has certain characteristics.

The first love of a man for a woman is the love that he has when he is young, fresh, pure, innocent, passionate, full of faith, full of zeal, blindness and even madness. All these qualities of love will drive you to the fulfilment of your divine call to ministry.

Indeed, without any special vision, any special dream, any supernatural voice, your love for God alone will carry you into His perfect will and ensure that you do all that He has called you to do.

How Love Guides You into the Will of God

1. Love tells you that you cannot wait till you are old.

Love makes you act NOW. When you are filled with love for God, you will not need to have a meeting to know when you are supposed to act. When a man loves a woman, he does not need to have a meeting and a discussion to know what to do or when to do it. He wants to do everything immediately. He wants to marry her immediately and take her to his home immediately. Having love for God and following this love will make the timing of your ministry accurate. God expects you to love Him. He loved you first and He is expecting you to respond to His love.

Can you imagine a twenty-three year old girl who says she loves you and will marry you only when she is in her fifties? If she has love for you, it will be most obvious that she must act now and not when she is fifty. So many young men say they love the Lord, but they will only throw themselves into His work when they cross the age of fifty. Do they really love the Lord? Love makes you act now!

> **Go and cry in the ears of Jerusalem, saying, Thus saith the LORD; I REMEMBER THEE, THE KINDNESS OF THY YOUTH, the love of thine espousals, when thou wentest after me in the wilderness, in a land that was not sown.**
>
> **Jeremiah 2:2**

2. Love tells you to follow God when you are pure and innocent.

You will fulfil your ministry by loving God when you are pure and innocent. First love is the love you have for God when you are pure. Following God in your innocence is a sign of your love for Him.

> **Seeing ye have purified your souls in obeying the truth through the Spirit unto unfeigned love of the brethren, see that ye love one another with a pure heart fervently:**
>
> **1 Peter 1:22**

3. Love tells you to serve God with passion and energy.

Love is stronger than death; it is stronger than jealousy. Love has a stronger flame than the flame of jealousy. When you love God you will be passionate and fiery. When a man loves a woman, he burns with passion towards her. When you love God, you will burn with passion towards Him.

> **But I say to the unmarried and to widows that it is good for them if they remain even as I. But if they do not have self-control, let them marry; for it is better to marry than to BURN WITH PASSION.**
>
> **1 Corinthians 7:8-9 (NASB)**

> **Set me as a seal upon thine heart, as a seal upon thine arm: for LOVE is strong as death; jealousy is cruel as the grave: the coals thereof are coals of fire, which HATH A MOST VEHEMENT FLAME.**
>
> **Song of Solomon 8:6**

4. Love tells you not to be afraid.

> **There is no fear in love; but perfect love casteth out fear: because fear hath torment. He that feareth is not made perfect in love.**
>
> **1 John 4:18**

If you follow your love for God, you will walk away from fear. Fear is an evil spirit that will guide you to hell. If you love God, you will not take decisions based on fear. Your perfect love will cast out fear. When a man loves a woman, he is not afraid to marry her and sign up to be with her for the rest of his life. Older people, however, have more fears because they may have been married before. Many older individuals are unable to love anyone because they are afraid their lives will be destroyed by the person they link up with. "Why should I marry this girl?" they would say. "She may hinder my ministry and destroy my life." Fear holds them back. Fear is very different from love. Your great love for God will guide you to take decisions without fear of tomorrow, fear of the future and fear of the unknown.

5. Love tells you to be zealous and energetic.

I am become a stranger unto my brethren, and an alien unto my mother's children. For the ZEAL OF THINE HOUSE HATH EATEN ME UP; and the reproaches of them that reproached thee are fallen upon me.

Psalms 69:8-9

Young couples that are passionately in love do not have to be advised to be zealous and energetic. It is older couples that are tired of each other who have to take vitamins and energy drinks to stir up their zeal. When you are filled with love for God, nothing will tell you to be zealous. You do not need to have a meeting where you will be told how you need to exert your energy for the Lord. When you love someone, you are naturally full of zeal.

6. Love does not have evil thoughts.

And she said unto him, How canst thou say, I love thee, when thine heart is not with me? Thou hast mocked me these three times, and hast not told me wherein thy great strength lieth. And it came to pass, when she pressed him daily with her words, and urged him, so that his soul was vexed unto death; That he told her all his heart, and said unto her, There hath not come a

razor upon mine head; for I have been a Nazarite unto God from my mother's womb: if I be shaven, then my strength will go from me, and I shall become weak, and be like any other man.

Judges 16:15-17

Samson never had evil thoughts about Delilah. That is why he allowed himself to relax with her. When you love God, you will not have any evil thoughts about God. You will be relaxed in His presence. You will be relaxed in the presence of God's servant. You will not have negative thoughts and questions about everything. Adam and Eve entertained evil thoughts about God. Adam and Eve allowed the devil to suggest that God was depriving them of some wonderful trees that they could have enjoyed.

7. **Love makes you do things that make people think you are mad.**

There be three things which are too wonderful for me, yea, four which I know not: The way of an eagle in the air; the way of a serpent upon a rock; the way of a ship in the midst of the sea; and the way of a man with a maid.

Proverbs 30:18-19

When a man is in love, people cannot advise him on what the right thing to do is. He almost seems mad because of the love that is so strong in his heart. I remember a couple in my church who were just sixteen years old. No one could advise them to break up their relationship. Even when they seemed to agree that they were too young, they continued in the madness of their love.

When you have first love for God, you will not need to have discussions about the will of God. Your passionate love will make you go out and do 'mad things' for Jesus. You will go out and bring others to God! You will pray for people to be saved! You will lead them to Christ!

You may be a student, but you will still serve God. People may suggest that you wait till you finish your studies. People said to me, "Brother Dag, take your time!" But my love for God could not allow me to slow down.

Your love for God will guide you on to a higher purpose. When I was a student, I did not need to have a vision, a dream or a voice to know what to do. My love for God told me to start a fellowship. My love for God told me to go preaching in the different halls of residence. My love for God made me fast. My love for God made me pray for hours. Love for God is a wonderful revelation and guide for your life and ministry. Your love for God will definitely guide you to make full proof of the ministry.

CHAPTER 7

Respond to the Mercy of God

Therefore seeing we have this ministry, as we have received MERCY, we faint not;

2 Corinthians 4:1

Respond to the mercy of God and you will make full proof of your ministry! Responding to the mercy of God is to walk in the supernatural path to the fulfilment of your ministry. Have a proper respect for the mercy that you have received. Have a proper respect for the mercy that God has shown you. As you respond to the mercy of God, you will definitely make full proof of your ministry!

To receive mercy is to experience the forgiveness that is shown to an offender.

God calling you means that He is being lenient with you and is having pity on you!

Honestly, there is no good reason for God to call you or use you. Your past is too abominable and you are too worthless for Him. There is no greater kindness than for God to stretch out His hand to someone like you or me. After salvation, God's greatest act of forgiveness, kindness and love to you, is His call.

Most of us do not think deeply about how evil we really are. If it occurred to us about how absolutely worthless and wicked we really were, we would be stunned into disbelief that God would want to work with somebody like us. Don't say things like, "Dear God, you will need to wait till I am 40 years old," or "Dear God, you will need to wait till I have finished my PhD." Doesn't it sound absurd to you? You are a wicked man! You are a dirty woman! Your presence in His house would cause a bad odour! Why would God want to work with a filthy person like you! Why don't you fall onto the ground and worship God for having suggested that somebody like you should work in His house?

> **And I THANK CHRIST JESUS our Lord, who hath enabled me, for that he counted me faithful, PUTTING ME INTO THE MINISTRY; who was before a blasphemer, and a persecutor, and injurious: but I OBTAINED MERCY, because I did it ignorantly in unbelief.**
>
> **1 Timothy 1:12-13**

Apostle Paul was so grateful that he had been allowed into the ministry. He knew that he had been a terrible person. His whole ministry was guided by the mercy that he had received. When you have been shown much love, you do not need to have meetings and discussions to know what to do. It will come naturally. You will respond, you will jump, you will be excited, you will set aside your inhibitions and show how grateful you are.

Why don't you start jumping, being excited and setting aside your inhibitions and show God how grateful you are to Him for calling you? Are you still seeking to know the will of God? The will of God is clear. Respond to the mercy that has been shown you. Be excited, set aside your reservations and love God unreservedly.

> **For I am the least of the apostles, that am not meet to be called an apostle, because I persecuted the church of God. But by the grace of God I am what I am: and his grace which was bestowed upon me was not in vain; but I LABOURED MORE ABUNDANTLY THAN THEY ALL: yet not I, but the grace of God which was with me.**
>
> **1 Corinthians 15:9-10**

What is your response when you are shown great grace and forgiveness? What was Paul's response? His response was to love God and serve Him more than others did. Paul knew that he had laboured more than all the other apostles. The other apostles had not been blasphemers. They had not been injurious to the church. Apostle Paul was the blasphemer who had received mercy. His response was to labour more abundantly than anyone else. That must be your response when you see that God has shown kindness to you.

If you respond to the grace of God and the mercy of God in the right way, you will instantly be in the will of God. You will find yourself in the centre of God's will, doing His pleasure. You will not make full proof of your ministry if you do not respond to the mercy of God properly.

CHAPTER 8

Accept Separation

At that time THE LORD SEPARATED THE TRIBE OF LEVI, to bear the ark of the covenant of the LORD, TO STAND BEFORE THE LORD TO MINISTER unto him, and to bless in his name, unto this day.

Deuteronomy 10:8

Accept "separation" and you will make full proof of your ministry! Accepting "separation" from other people is to walk in the supernatural path that leads to the fulfilment of your ministry. Appreciate how God is separating you from so many other people. Have a proper respect for God's decision to separate you from others. As you flow along with 'separation' and the separated life of a minister, you will definitely make full proof of your ministry!

You can only fulfil your ministry by deeply understanding the separation that God has caused to take place between you and other people just like you. When you accept the separation and flow in it, you will fulfil a large aspect of your ministry.

To be "called" by God means to be separated for His purposes. Perhaps, this is the most important definition of what it means to be "called". God's calling isolates you and separates you from the larger body of Christians. To be separated means to detach somebody from a larger group. Your calling therefore means that you have been isolated for the purposes of God.

Your calling means you have been separated from the larger society of Christians. Separation speaks of being severed from an association. To be separated means that you have been withdrawn from something. In this case, you have been withdrawn from secular life, secular ideals and secular goals. By your calling, you have been separated from your family and friends. Indeed, a high calling may even mean that you have been separated from other Christians.

> **The sons of Amram; Aaron and Moses: and AARON WAS SEPARATED, that he should sanctify the most holy things, he and his sons for ever, to burn incense before the LORD, to minister unto him, and to bless in his name for ever.**
>
> **1 Chronicles 23:13**

In the Old Testament, the Hebrew word translated 'separate' is *badal*, which means to distinguish and make a difference between you and others. Is it not a blessing that God has distinguished between you and others? He has made a difference between you and other believers! What else can you ask for?

In the New Testament, the Greek word for separate is *aphorizo,* which also means to keep apart two or more people by a boundary. God is keeping you apart and has put a boundary between you and the rest. What higher blessing could you hope for than for God to keep you apart for His special purposes? Notice how Paul described his ministry as a separation from others;

Paul, a servant of Jesus Christ, called to be an apostle, SEPARATED UNTO THE GOSPEL of God,

Romans 1:1

As they ministered to the Lord, and fasted, the Holy Ghost said, SEPARATE ME BARNABAS AND SAUL for the work whereunto I have called them.

Acts 13:2

It is time for you to accept that God is putting a boundary between you and others. God has decided to use you greatly. Do not try to belong to company that God is separating you from. Do not try to be like your old school friends. Do not try to be like your brothers and sisters. Do not try to be like your colleagues from your secular office. Do not try to be like the rest of your family. *ACCEPT SEPARATION!*

It is not easy to be separated from your family, friends, colleagues and classmates. When I finished medical school, I had fifty-four other classmates who went on to acquire higher and greater medical laurels. I was left behind and completely separated from all my colleagues and mates. It was not a nice feeling to be left behind. I did not want to be left behind and I did not want to be separated.

My new friends and colleagues were people who had never been in my class. From 1989, when I looked over my shoulder, I realised God had separated me from my classmates.

"Separation" is a real part of being called to the ministry. People who insist on hanging on and being close to people God is separating them from, often lose their ministry. Flowing with "separation" leads you into the centre of God's will. Flowing with "separation" will enable you to make full proof of your ministry.

God can separate you from an entire nation. When I was growing up, people like me went to certain schools and did certain things. Most of my childhood friends had European parents who were friends of my mother. When I gave my life to Jesus, I became completely separated from that group of people. I now had new friends who had no such background. Flowing with the "separation" that came to me helped me to step into the very centre of God's will.

Abraham in the 'School of Separation'

> **Now the Lord had said unto Abram, Get thee out of thy country, and from thy kindred, and from thy father's house, unto a land that I will shew thee: And I will make of thee a great nation, and I will bless thee, and make thy name great; and thou shalt be a blessing:**
>
> **Genesis 12:1-2**

When you are so proud of your nation, your people and the background that God is separating you from, you are unable to disconnect and accept a new family. There is much to be learnt in the new family that God is separating you into. When God called Abraham, He wanted him to move away from his family, his relatives and their ways. Abraham's family was an idol-worshipping family. God wanted Abraham to serve the living God. To do that, Abraham had to separate himself from his idol-worshipping clan.

All the problems and crises of Abraham's life can be traced to Abraham taking one of the people he was supposed to be separated from, along with him. "So Abram departed, as the Lord had spoken unto him; and Lot went with him: and Abram was seventy and five years old when he departed out of Haran" (Genesis 12:4). God never intended Abraham to take Lot with him. God actually told Abraham to separate from all his family members. Abraham did not obey God fully and opened the door to demonic attacks and various types of crises. Abraham had to fight wars because he did not separate from Lot. Abraham had a lot of strife because he did not separate from Lot. Accept to be separate and you will be delivered from major problems in this life.

The wars that Abraham fought were fought to rescue Lot:

> And they took Lot, Abram's brother's son, who dwelt in Sodom, and his goods, and departed. And there came one that had escaped, and told Abram the Hebrew; for he dwelt in the plain of Mamre the Amorite, brother of Eshcol, and brother of Aner: and these were confederate with Abram.
>
> And when Abram heard that his brother was taken captive, he armed his trained servants, born in his own house, three hundred and eighteen, and pursued them unto Dan.
>
> Genesis 14:12-14

The intercessions of Abraham were because of Lot:

> And Abraham drew near, and said, Wilt thou also destroy the righteous with the wicked? Peradventure there be fifty righteous within the city: wilt thou also destroy and not spare the place for the fifty righteous that are therein?
>
> Genesis 18:23-24

The strife of Abraham was because of Lot:

The strife that Abraham experienced in his camp came from quarrels between Abraham's herdsmen and Lot's herdsmen.

> And there was a strife between the herdmen of Abram's cattle and the herdmen of Lot's cattle: and the Canaanite and the Perizzite dwelled then in the land.
>
> And Abram said unto Lot, Let there be no strife, I pray thee, between me and thee, and between my herdmen and thy herdmen; for we be brethren.
>
> Genesis 13:7-8

You will avoid these three major crises of your life and ministry if you accept to flow with what God is separating you from.

CHAPTER 9

Seek Out the Mystery of the Will of God

He made known to us THE MYSTERY OF HIS WILL, according to His kind intention which He purposed in Him.

Ephesians 1:9

Seek out the mystery of the will of God and you will make full proof of your ministry! Seeking out the mystery of the will of God will lead you on the supernatural path to the fulfilment of your ministry. Have a proper respect for the mysterious nature of the will of God. As you continually seek to know the mystery of His will, you will make full proof of your ministry!

You can only fulfil your ministry by understanding that the will of God is a mystery. Once you accept that God's will is mysterious, you will have a proper respect for it and you will pray about it. Jesus prayed very often about the will of God. The will of God is a mystery.

What it Means for the Will of God to be a Mystery

1. The will of God for your ministry is a mystery because it is UNKNOWN.

Many of the things God has intended to do with your life are unknown. Without spending hours praying for the will of God to be done, much of it will never be realised. You simply cannot tell what God has planned for your ministry. Why do you think Jesus spent so much time praying that the will of the Father be done?

2. The will of God for your ministry is a mystery because it is a SECRET.

A mystery is a secret that has not yet been revealed. What God will do in your life is a secret. I had no idea that I would ever write a book. It had been kept secret for me. I had no idea that I would plant many churches. I had no idea that I would have a worldwide ministry. All these things had been kept secret from me. I know that other things that God has planned have been kept secret from me. It is my duty to pray and wait on Him for the mystery of His will to be revealed to me. By waiting on God to find out these secrets I will make full proof of my ministry.

3. The will of God for your life is a mystery because it is UNEXPLAINED and PUZZLING.

The will of God is puzzling, to say the least. If you think you will understand all the things that are contained in the will of God, then you do not know God. Much of the will of God does not follow our logic. As far as the heavens are above the earth, so are His ways and His thoughts above our ways. People you think will live long lives may die leaving you confused. People you think should live short lives may live on and on, leaving you puzzled. Ministers you disapprove of may seem to have God's approval. Ministers you have written off as fallen may rise and flourish, in spite of the fact that they you may despise them.

4. The will of God for your ministry is a mystery because it REQUIRES A DIVINE REVELATION.

The will of God requires a divine revelation. It is impossible to know the will of God by thinking logically. I once asked the Lord what to do in order to bear fruit. I thought God was going to tell me to build more churches. I suddenly saw a vision of a hand holding a book. I knew that mysteriously, the books were my key to bearing fruit. Without waiting on the Lord and praying about His will, you may never see large sections of His will for your life unfold.

5. The will of God for your ministry is a mystery because it REQUIRES YOU TO PRAY.

This makes the will of God even more mysterious.

...Thy will be done in earth, as it is in heaven.

Matthew 6:10

It is very mysterious that we even have to pray about the will of God.

Jesus taught us to pray for the will of God to be done. Why should we have to pray for the will of God to be done? Can't the will of God just happen spontaneously?

When Jesus was in the Garden of Gethsemane, He spent three hours praying for the will of God to be done. Why did He have to pray for three hours, saying "Let thy will be done"? Is it so hard for the will of God to materialise? Does God not have the whole world in His hand? Is there anything happening in this world that is not the will of God? If God is so great, does He not just ensure that His will and plan work out?

> **And he went a little further, and fell on his face, and prayed, saying, O my Father, if it be possible, let this cup pass from me: nevertheless not as I will, but as thou wilt.**
>
> **Matthew 26:39**

The prayer in the Garden of Gethsemane is one of the most significant prayers for anyone who wants to be successful in ministry. You need to pray to the Lord for all the secrets, unknown things, hidden treasures of your ministry to come out and manifest themselves. After Jesus prayed that prayer, all the events that unfolded led to His crucifixion. The perfect will of God was done. There was no mistake and no error because he had prayed.

> **For this reason also, since the day we heard of it, we have not ceased to pray for you and to ask that you may be filled with the knowledge of His will in all spiritual wisdom and understanding,**
>
> **Colossians 1:9**

CHAPTER 10

Obey Your Specific Call

Paul, a servant of Jesus Christ, called to be an apostle, separated unto the gospel of God.

Romans 1:1

Obey your specific call and you will make full proof of your ministry! Obeying your specific calling is to walk in the supernatural path to the fulfilment of your ministry. Have a proper respect for the call of God. Have a proper respect for the fact that the call of God is highly specific. As you respond to the specific call of God, you will most certainly make full proof of your ministry!

You can only make full proof of your ministry by knowing and accepting that you are called by God. If you believe in the call of God, you will live your life in great fear of this truth that God has called you to serve Him in a special way. Accepting the call of God is the next important step to make full proof of your ministry.

> **Now the word of the Lord came unto Jonah the son of Amittai, saying, Arise, go to Nineveh, that great city, and cry against it; for their wickedness is come up before me. But Jonah rose up to flee unto Tarshish from the presence of the Lord, and went down to Joppa; and he found a ship going to Tarshish: so he paid the fare thereof, and went down into it, to go with them unto Tarshish from the presence of the Lord.**
>
> **Jonah 1:1-3**

1. The call of God is a door through which you enter ministry.

Other jobs require certificates from school, recommendations from important people and connections in life. Unfortunately, there are no connections that can get you into the ministry. There are no certificates that can help you to get into real ministry. No one can really recommend you in such a way that you will be launched into your ministry. Sometimes, if your father knows someone, it can help you to get a job. In ministry however, you must enter through the call! Some people call that a divine inspiration.

2. If God has called you, shout and jump for joy!

You have been summoned to the highest kind of job to work for no one other than King Jesus! If God has called you, you have received a genuine entrance into God's work. Actually, God does not need you to accomplish anything on earth. You desperately need to be chosen for something honourable in this life. You must see the call of God as a specific mission that you have been given. You must strive to hear from God and follow what He says.

3. Don't call yourself. Be sure that you are called.

Remember, the only way into ministry is a call! All through my life I have battled with my thoughts as to whether I was really called. Why have I battled within? Because no man can take this honour unto himself (Hebrews 5:4). No man can call himself! No one should call himself! Ministry must wait until there is a definite call. Once you have been called, you are standing on a solid foundation. It is a bit like a girl getting married. She cannot propose to a man. She has to wait until a man proposes to her. If she enters into her marriage through her own proposal, her husband will always feel uncertain as to whether he married her or she married him! He will say, "She chased me. She forced me. She manipulated me and that's how come I married her."

4. No one else has your calling.

Some people think there is only one girl they can ever marry. Some people think there is one person in the world who is created for them. I cannot tell whether that is the case. However, when it comes to the ministry, be aware that the call is very specific. The call of God is a specific commission that God has for you. No one in the Bible had the commission that Jonah had. He is the only one who was sent to Nineveh. You must see yourself as someone with a specific mission that only you can accomplish.

5. Your call is without repentance.

> And the word of the Lord came unto Jonah the second time, saying, arise, go unto Nineveh, that great city, and preach unto it the preaching that I bid thee.
>
> Jonah 3:1-2

You must notice how Jonah's call did not change even though he ran away from it. Why didn't God search for another person? If the message was so urgent, why didn't He raise up another prophet to do his work? Why did God insist on using someone who was clearly disobedient and stubborn? Why did God insist on using a disobedient person to warn others about disobedience? I can't really tell. Most of us would have given up on Jonah when he was swallowed by the whale. The gifts and calling of God are without repentance (Romans 11:29). God does not change His mind about what He has called you to do. When He called you, He was giving you a privilege. A call is basically a privilege. It is not a job. It is an honour! It is a promotion! In my language, we would say it is an '*onaporific opportunity*'.

CHAPTER 11

Go on Your Mission!

But the Lord said unto me, say not, I am a child: FOR THOU SHALT GO TO ALL THAT I SHALL SEND THEE, and whatsoever I command thee thou shalt speak.

Jeremiah 1:7

Go on your mission! Go ye therefore! Go where you are sent and you will make full proof of your ministry! Going where you are sent is to walk in the supernatural path to the fulfilment of your ministry. Have a proper respect for the mission you have received. Going where you are sent shows a proper respect for God. Humbly accepting the mission field is very important for making full proof of your ministry. As you go where you are sent, you will definitely make full proof of your ministry!

You can only make full proof of your ministry by going where you are sent. If you believed you were called of God, you would definitely be sent to do something for Him. It is this first assignment that is your mission. A mission is not only when you are sent to another country. To be on a mission is to be sent to accomplish a specific task for God.

To be on a mission is to go where you are sent. There is a difference between someone who was sent and someone who just went! God sending you means He is dispatching you on a journey to serve Him or to get something done for Him. Indeed, God is sending you to fetch many souls from the grips of the devil.

Some people want to choose where they would like to go. Some people want to go where there is money, riches and apparent prosperity. Some people want to go where they think they will prosper. That is not the key to making full proof of your ministry. The key to success in ministry is to go where you are sent. Do not ask to be sent to any particular place. Go where you are asked to go. That is the key to maximum impact in ministry.

The Hebrew word for 'sent' is *shalach*, which means to send someone away. The call of God often means that you will be sent away from your family and friends. In the Greek, the word 'sent' is *apostello*, which means to set someone apart and to send someone out properly on a mission. Many people are not sent out properly and this affects their entire ministry.

John the Baptist was a man sent by God and Jesus said of him that there was no one greater. It is a great thing to be sent! To make full proof of your ministry, you must go where you are sent! Allow God to send you anywhere to do anything!

There was A MAN SENT FROM GOD, whose name was John.

John 1:6

Jesus Christ is the best example of someone who went where He was sent. He came to this earth full of wicked people and lived amongst us to preach the gospel. Jesus Himself said that He had been sent. If Jesus were to have chosen where to go, He would not have chosen to come to this earth. This whole world lies in wickedness. This world is full of demons, para-humans, fallen men, greedy and selfish human beings, lust-filled nations and disease-plagued humanity. Earth is not a nice place to be sent to.

The Spirit of the Lord is upon me, because he hath anointed me to preach the gospel to the poor; HE HATH SENT ME to heal the brokenhearted, to preach deliverance to the captives, and recovering of sight to the blind, to set at liberty them that are bruised,

Luke 4:18

Jesus saith unto them, my meat is to do the will of HIM THAT SENT ME, and to finish his work.

John 4:34

The key to maximum impact is to go where you are sent to go. It is the key to making full proof of your ministry. Going willingly is a great key. If you are willing and obedient you will eat the fruit of the land (Isaiah 1:19). The reason why some missionaries do not enjoy the nations they are sent to, is because even though they are *obedient*, they are not *willing*. This could be the reason why some singers do not sing well when they are asked to sing certain songs. They may sing in *obedience* but they do not sing *willingly*. Anything that you obey unwillingly does not yield great fruit.

Twenty-Five People who Made Full Proof of Their Ministry When they Were Sent by God

1. NOAH WENT ON A MISSION TO BUILD AN ARK:

AND GOD SAID UNTO NOAH, The end of all flesh is come before me; for the earth is filled with violence through them; and, behold, I will destroy them with the earth.

MAKE THEE AN ARK of gopher wood; rooms shalt thou make in the ark, and shalt pitch it within and without with pitch.

Genesis 6:13-14

2. ABRAHAM WENT ON A MISSION OUT OF HIS COUNTRY AND AWAY FROM HIS RELATIVES:

Now the Lord had said unto Abram, GET THEE OUT OF THY COUNTRY, and from thy kindred, and from thy father's house, unto a land that I will shew thee:

Genesis 12:1

3. JACOB WAS SENT ON A MISSION TO LIVE IN BETHEL:

And GOD SAID UNTO JACOB, ARISE, GO UP TO BETHEL, AND DWELL THERE: and make there an altar unto God, that appeared unto thee when thou fleddest from the face of Esau thy brother.

Then Jacob said unto his household, and to all that were with him, Put away the strange gods that are among you, and be clean, and change your garments: And let us arise, and go up to Bethel; and I will make there an altar unto God, who answered me in the day of my distress, and was with me in the way which I went.

Genesis 35:1-3

4. GIDEON WAS SENT ON A MISSION TO SAVE ISRAEL FROM THE MIDIANITES:

And Gideon said unto him, Oh my Lord, if the Lord be with us, why then is all this befallen us? And where be all his miracles which our fathers told us of, saying, did not the Lord bring us up from Egypt? But now the Lord hath forsaken us, and delivered us into the hands of the Midianites.

And the Lord looked upon him, and said, go in this thy might, and thou shalt save Israel from the hand of the Midianites: HAVE NOT I SENT THEE?

Judges 6:13-14

5. THE TWO SPIES WERE SENT ON A MISSION TO SPY OUT THE LAND OF JERICHO:

Then JOSHUA THE SON OF NUN SENT TWO MEN AS SPIES secretly from Shittim, saying, "Go, view the land, especially Jericho." So they went and came into the house of a harlot whose name was Rahab, and lodged there.

Joshua 2:1 (NASB)

6. FIVE SPIES OF DAN WERE SENT ON A MISSION TO SPY OUT THE LAND:

In those days there was no king in Israel: and in those days the tribe of the Danites sought them an inheritance to dwell in; for unto that day all their inheritance had not fallen unto them among the tribes of Israel. And the children of Dan sent of their family FIVE MEN from their coasts, Men of valour, from Zorah, and from Eshtaol, to spy out the land, and to search it; and they said unto them, GO, SEARCH THE LAND: who when they came to mount Ephraim, to the house of Micah, they lodged there.

Judges 18:1-2

7. SAUL WAS SENT ON A MISSION TO DESTROY THE AMALEKITES:

And the Lord sent thee on a journey, and said, go and utterly destroy the sinners the Amalekites, and fight against them until they be consumed.

1 Samuel 15:18

8. PROPHET NATHAN WAS SENT ON A MISSION TO SPEAK TO THE KING:

AND THE LORD SENT NATHAN UNTO DAVID. And he came unto him, and said unto him, There were two men in one city; the one rich, and the other poor.

2 Samuel 12:1

9. ISAAC WAS SENT ON A MISSION TO LIVE IN GERAR:

And the Lord appeared unto him, and said, go not down into Egypt; dwell in the land which I shall tell thee of: SOJOURN IN THIS LAND, and I will be with thee, and will bless thee; for unto thee, and unto thy seed, I will give all these countries, and I will perform the oath which I sware unto Abraham thy father;

Genesis 26:2-3

10. JOSEPH WAS SENT ON A MISSION TO EGYPT TO PRESERVE HIS BRETHREN:

Now therefore be not grieved, nor angry with yourselves, that ye sold me hither: for GOD DID SEND ME BEFORE YOU TO PRESERVE LIFE.

Genesis 45: 5

11. MOSES WAS SENT ON A MISSION TO SPEAK TO PHARAOH:

COME NOW THEREFORE, AND I WILL SEND THEE UNTO PHARAOH, that thou mayest bring forth my people the children of Israel out of Egypt.

Exodus 3:10

12. TWELVE SPIES WERE SENT ON A MISSION TO SPY THE LAND OF CANAAN:

Then the LORD spoke to Moses saying, "Send out for yourself men so that they may spy out the land of Canaan, which I am going to give to the sons of Israel; you shall send a man from each of their fathers' tribes, every one a leader among them."

So Moses sent them from the wilderness of Paran at the command of the LORD, all of them men who were heads of the sons of Israel.

Numbers 13:1-3 (NASB)

13. SAMUEL WAS SENT ON A MISSION TO ANOINT SAUL AS KING:

Samuel also said unto Saul, THE LORD SENT ME TO ANOINT THEE to be king over his people, over Israel: now therefore hearken thou unto the voice of the words of the Lord.

1 Samuel 15:1

14. ELIJAH WAS SENT ON A MISSION TO HIDE:

And the word of the Lord came unto him, saying, get thee hence, and turn thee eastward, and hide thyself by the brook Cherith, that is before Jordan.

1 Kings 17:2-3

15. ELIJAH WAS SENT ON A MISSION TO A WIDOW:

And the word of the Lord came unto him, saying, arise, get thee to Zarephath, which belongeth to Zidon, and dwell there: behold, I have commanded a widow woman there to sustain thee.

1 Kings 17:8-9

16. A PROPHET WAS SENT ON A MISSION TO REBUKE KING AMAZIAH:

Now after Amaziah came from slaughtering the Edomites, he brought the gods of the sons of Seir, set them up as his gods, bowed down before them and burned incense to them.

Then the anger of the Lord burned against Amaziah, and HE SENT HIM A PROPHET WHO SAID TO HIM, "why have you sought the gods of the people who have not delivered their own people from your hand?"

As he was talking with him, the king said to him, "Have we appointed you a royal counselor? Stop! Why should you be struck down?" Then the prophet stopped and said, I know that God has planned to destroy you, because you have done this and have not listened to my counsel."

2 Chronicles 25:14-16 (NASB)

17. ESTHER WAS SENT ON A MISSION TO RESCUE THE JEWS:

For if thou altogether holdest thy peace at this time, then shall there enlargement and deliverance arise to the Jews from another place; but thou and thy father's house shall be destroyed: and WHO KNOWETH WHETHER THOU ART COME TO THE KINGDOM FOR SUCH A TIME AS THIS?

Esther 4:14

18. ISAIAH WAS SENT ON A MISSION TO GIVE A MESSAGE TO THE PEOPLE OF ISRAEL:

Also I heard the voice of the Lord, saying, whom shall I send, and who will go for us? Then said I, Here am I; send me.

AND HE SAID, GO, AND TELL THIS PEOPLE, Hear ye indeed, but understand not; and see ye indeed, but perceive not.

Make the heart of this people fat, and make their ears heavy, and shut their eyes; lest they see with their eyes, and hear with their ears, and understand with their heart, and convert, and be healed.

Isaiah 6:8-10

19. PROPHET JEREMIAH WAS SENT ON A MISSION TO THE NATIONS:

Then the word of the Lord came unto me, saying, before I formed thee in the belly I knew thee; and before thou camest forth out of the womb I sanctified thee, and I ORDAINED THEE A PROPHET UNTO THE NATIONS.

Jeremiah 1:4-5

20. EZEKIEL WAS SENT ON A MISSION TO REBUKE THE SHEPHERDS OF ISRAEL:

And the word of the Lord came unto me, saying, son of man, PROPHESY AGAINST THE SHEPHERDS of Israel, prophesy, and say unto them, thus saith the Lord God unto the shepherds; woe be to the shepherds of Israel that do feed themselves! should not the shepherds feed the flocks?

Ezekiel 34:1-2

21. HOSEA WAS SENT ON A MISSION TO MARRY A PROSTITUTE:

The beginning of the word of the Lord by Hosea. And the Lord said to Hosea, GO, TAKE UNTO THEE A WIFE OF WHOREDOMS and children of whoredoms: for the land hath committed great whoredom, departing from the Lord.

Hosea 1:2

22. PHILIP WAS SENT ON A MISSION TO THE ETHIOPIAN EUNUCH:

Then the Spirit said unto Philip, GO NEAR, AND JOIN THYSELF TO THIS CHARIOT.

Acts 8:29

23. THE MAD MAN OF GADARA WAS SENT ON A MISSION TO TESTIFY OF JESUS CHRIST:

And He did not let him, but HE SAID TO HIM, "GO HOME TO YOUR PEOPLE AND REPORT to them what great things the Lord has done for you, and how He had mercy on you."

And he went away and began to proclaim in Decapolis what great things Jesus had done for him; and everyone was amazed.

Mark 5:19-20 (NASB)

24. BARNABAS AND SAUL WERE SENT ON A MISSION TO THE GENTILES:

Now there were in the church that was at Antioch certain prophets and teachers; as Barnabas, and Simeon that was called Niger, and Lucius of Cyrene, and Manaen, which had been brought up with Herod the tetrarch, and Saul.

As they ministered to the Lord, and fasted, the Holy Ghost said, Separate me Barnabas and Saul for the work whereunto I have called them.

And when they had fasted and prayed, and laid their hands on them, they sent them away.

So they, BEING SENT FORTH BY THE HOLY GHOST, departed unto Seleucia; and from thence they sailed to Cyprus.

Acts 13:1-4

25. JESUS WAS SENT ON A MISSION TO SAVE THE WORLD:

But when the fulness of the time was come, GOD SENT FORTH HIS SON, made of a woman, made under the law, to redeem them that were under the law, that we might receive the adoption of sons.

And because ye are sons, God hath sent forth the Spirit of his Son into your hearts, crying, Abba, Father.

Wherefore thou art no more a servant, but a son; and if a son, then an heir of God through Christ.

Galatians 4:4-7

In this was manifested the love of God toward us, because that GOD SENT HIS ONLY BEGOTTEN SON into the world, that we might live through Him.

Herein is love, not that we loved God, but that he loved us, and SENT HIS SON to be the propitiation for our sins.

1 John 4:9-10

CHAPTER 12

This is Where to Go and This is What to Preach

Go ye therefore, and teach all nations, baptizing them in the name of the Father, and of the Son, and of the Holy Ghost:

Teaching them to observe all things whatsoever I have commanded you: and, lo, I am with you alway, even unto the end of the world. Amen.

Matthew 28:19-20

Go where you are told to go! Preach what you are told to preach! If you go where you are told to go and preach what you are told to preach, you will make full proof of your ministry!

Preaching what you are told to preach is to walk in the supernatural path to the fulfilment of your ministry. Have a proper respect for the message God has given you and preach what you have been told to preach. As you are faithful with the message you have been asked to preach, you will definitely make full proof of your ministry!

Jonah was told where to go and he was told what to preach. That is the key to making full proof of your ministry. The key to total success in ministry is rooted in being told where to go and being told what to preach. You can expect to make the greatest impact in ministry when you go where you are told to go and when you preach what you are told to preach! I want you to remember these two phrases: "This is where to go…!", "This is what to preach…!"

The message you preach is very important. The message you preach can be compared to the type of food that is served in a restaurant. If you sell Ghanaian food in Korea, you are likely to have very few customers. If you serve Korean food in Ghana, you are likely to have very few customers.

This is why it is important to serve exactly what you are told to serve. This is why it is important to preach exactly what you are told to preach.

I want you to see a few examples of people who were told where to go and what to preach

JESUS CHRIST

1. THIS IS WHERE TO GO: JESUS CHRIST WAS TOLD WHERE TO GO.

> For God so loved the world, that he gave his only begotten Son, that whosoever believeth in him should not perish,

but have everlasting life. For GOD SENT not His Son INTO THE WORLD to condemn the world; but that the world through him might be saved.

John 3:16-17

2. THIS IS WHAT TO PREACH: JESUS CHRIST WAS TOLD WHAT TO PREACH

Then said Jesus unto them, when ye have lifted up the Son of man, then shall ye know that I am he, and that I do nothing of myself; but AS MY FATHER HATH TAUGHT ME, I SPEAK THESE THINGS.

John 8:28

3. JESUS CHRIST MADE FULL PROOF OF HIS MINISTRY

The Pharisees therefore said among themselves, Perceive ye how ye prevail nothing? behold, THE WORLD IS GONE AFTER HIM.

John 12:19

JOHN THE BAPTIST

1. THIS IS WHERE TO GO: JOHN THE BAPTIST WAS TOLD WHERE TO GO

There was A MAN SENT FROM GOD, whose name was John. The same came for a witness, to bear witness of the Light, that all men through him might believe. He was not that Light, but was sent to bear witness of that Light.

John 1:6-8

2. THIS IS WHAT TO PREACH: JOHN THE BAPTIST WAS TOLD WHAT TO PREACH

In those days came John the Baptist, preaching in the wilderness of Judaea, And saying, REPENT YE: FOR THE KINGDOM OF HEAVEN IS AT HAND. For this is he that was spoken of by the prophet Esaias, saying, The voice of one crying in the wilderness, Prepare ye the way of the Lord, make his paths straight.

Matthew 3:1-3

3. JOHN THE BAPTIST MADE FULL PROOF OF HIS MINISTRY

THEN WENT OUT TO HIM JERUSALEM, and all Judaea, and ALL THE REGION ROUND ABOUT JORDAN, and were baptized of him in Jordan, confessing their sins.

Matthew 3:5-6

JONAH

1. THIS IS WHERE TO GO: JONAH WAS TOLD WHERE TO GO

Now the word of the Lord came unto Jonah the son of Amittai, saying, arise, GO TO NINEVEH, that great city, and CRY AGAINST IT; for their wickedness is come up before me.

Jonah 1:1-2

2. THIS IS WHAT TO PREACH: JONAH WAS TOLD WHAT TO PREACH

And the word of the Lord came unto Jonah the second time, saying, Arise, go unto Nineveh, that great city, and PREACH UNTO IT THE PREACHING THAT I BID THEE. So Jonah arose, and went unto Nineveh, according to the word of the Lord. Now Nineveh was an exceeding great city of three days' journey. And Jonah began to enter into the city a day's journey, and he cried, and said, yet forty days, and Nineveh shall be overthrown.

Jonah 3:1-4

3. JONAH MADE FULL PROOF OF HIS MINISTRY

Jonah was a high impact shepherd because he went where he was told to go and he preached what he was told to preach.

So the people of Nineveh believed God, and proclaimed a fast, and put on sackcloth, from the greatest of them even to the least of them.

For word came unto THE KING of Nineveh, and he arose from his throne, and he laid his robe from him, and COVERED HIM WITH SACKCLOTH, AND SAT IN ASHES.

And he caused it to be proclaimed and published through Nineveh by the decree of the king and his nobles, saying, LET NEITHER MAN NOR BEAST, HERD NOR FLOCK, TASTE ANY THING: LET THEM NOT FEED, NOR DRINK WATER: BUT LET MAN AND BEAST BE COVERED WITH SACKCLOTH, AND CRY MIGHTILY UNTO GOD: yea, let them turn every one from his evil way, and from the violence that is in their hands.

Who can tell if God will turn and repent, and turn away from his fierce anger, that we perish not? And God saw their works, that they turned from their evil way; and God repented of the evil, that he had said that he would do unto them; and he did it not.

Jonah 3:5-10

ELIJAH

1. THIS IS WHERE TO GO: ELIJAH WAS TOLD WHERE TO GO.

And it came to pass after many days, that the word of the Lord came to Elijah in the third year, saying, GO, SHEW THYSELF UNTO AHAB; and I will send rain upon the earth.

1 Kings 18:1

2. THIS IS WHAT TO PREACH: ELIJAH WAS TOLD WHAT TO PREACH.

And the word of the Lord came to Elijah the Tishbite, saying, arise, go down to meet Ahab king of Israel, which is in Samaria: behold, he is in the vineyard of Naboth, whither he is gone down to possess it

And THOU SHALT SPEAK UNTO HIM, SAYING, Thus saith the Lord, Hast thou killed, and also taken possession? And thou shalt speak unto him, saying, Thus saith the Lord, in the place where dogs licked the blood of Naboth shall dogs lick thy blood, even thine.

BEHOLD, I WILL BRING EVIL UPON THEE, AND WILL TAKE AWAY THY POSTERITY, and will cut off from Ahab him that pisseth against the wall, and him that is shut up and left in Israel, and will make thine house like the house of Jeroboam the son of Nebat, and like the house of Baasha the son of Ahijah, for the provocation wherewith thou hast provoked me to anger, and made Israel to sin.

And of Jezebel also spake the Lord, saying, The dogs shall eat Jezebel by the wall of Jezreel. Him that dieth of Ahab in the city the dogs shall eat; and him that dieth in the field shall the fowls of the air eat.

1 Kings 21:17-19, 21-24

3. ELIJAH MADE FULL PROOF OF HIS MINISTRY

And it came to pass, when Ahab heard those words, that HE RENT HIS CLOTHES, AND PUT SACKCLOTH UPON HIS FLESH, AND FASTED, AND LAY IN SACKCLOTH, AND WENT SOFTLY.

And the word of the Lord came to Elijah the Tishbite, saying, seest thou how Ahab humbleth himself before me? Because he humbleth himself before me, I will not bring the evil in his days: but in his son's days will I bring the evil upon his house.

1 Kings 21:27-29

THE MAN OF GOD FROM JUDAH

1. **THIS IS WHERE TO GO: THE MAN OF GOD FROM JUDAH WAS TOLD WHERE TO GO.**

AT THE LORD'S COMMAND, A MAN OF GOD FROM JUDAH WENT TO BETHEL, arriving there just as Jeroboam was approaching the altar to burn incense.

1 Kings 13: 1 (NLT)

2. **THIS IS WHAT TO PREACH: THE MAN OF GOD FROM JUDAH WAS TOLD WHAT TO PREACH.**

Then AT THE LORD'S COMMAND, HE SHOUTED, "O altar, altar! This is what the Lord says: A child named Josiah will be born into the dynasty of David. On you he will sacrifice the priests from the pagan shrines who come here to burn incense, and human bones will be burned on you.

1 Kings 13: 2 (NLT)

3. **THE MAN OF GOD FROM JUDAH MADE FULL PROOF OF HIS MINISTRY.**

That same day the man of God gave a sign to prove his message. He said, "The Lord has promised to give this sign: this altar will split apart, and its ashes will be poured out on the ground."

When King Jeroboam heard the man of God speaking against the altar at Bethel, he pointed at him and shouted, "Seize that man!" BUT INSTANTLY THE KING'S HAND BECAME PARALYZED IN THAT POSITION, and he couldn't pull it back. At the same time a wide crack appeared in the altar, and the ashes poured out, just as the man of God had predicted in his message from the Lord.

The king cried out to the man of God, "Please ask the Lord your God to restore my hand again!" So the man of God prayed to the Lord, and the king's hand was restored and he could move it again.

1 Kings 13: 3-6 (NLT)

TIMOTHY

1. THIS IS WHERE TO GO: TIMOTHY WAS TOLD WHERE TO GO.

As I BESOUGHT THEE TO ABIDE STILL AT EPHESUS, when I went into Macedonia, that thou mightest charge some that they teach no other doctrine,

1 Timothy 1:3

2. THIS IS WHAT TO PREACH: TIMOTHY WAS TOLD WHAT TO PREACH.

Timothy basically preached what Paul told him to preach.

As I besought thee to abide still at Ephesus, when I went into Macedonia, that thou mightest charge some that they teach no other doctrine, Neither give heed to fables and endless genealogies, which minister questions, rather than godly edifying which is in faith: so do.

1 Timothy 1:3-4

And the things that thou hast heard of me among many witnesses, the same commit thou to faithful men, who shall be able to teach others also.

2 Timothy 2:2

Of these things put them in remembrance, charging them before the Lord that they strive not about words to no profit, but to the subverting of the hearers.

2 Timothy 2:14

Preach the word; be instant in season, out of season; reprove, rebuke, exhort with all longsuffering and doctrine. For the time will come when they will not endure sound doctrine; but after their own lusts shall they heap to themselves teachers, having itching ears; and they shall turn away their ears from the truth, and shall be turned unto fables. But watch thou in all things, endure afflictions, do the work of an evangelist, make full proof of thy ministry.

2 Timothy 4:2-5

3. TIMOTHY MADE FULL PROOF OF HIS MINISTRY.

But watch thou in all things, endure afflictions, do the work of an evangelist, make FULL PROOF of thy ministry.

2 Timothy 4:5

TITUS

1. THIS IS WHERE TO GO: TITUS WAS TOLD WHERE TO GO.

For this cause left I THEE IN CRETE, that thou shouldest set in order the things that are wanting, and ordain elders in every city, as I had appointed thee:

Titus 1:5

2. THIS IS WHAT TO PREACH: TITUS WAS TOLD WHAT TO PREACH.

But SPEAK THOU THE THINGS WHICH BECOME SOUND DOCTRINE:

That the aged men be sober, grave, temperate, sound in faith, in charity, in patience.

The aged women likewise, that they be in behaviour as becometh holiness, not false accusers, not given to much wine, teachers of good things; That they may teach the young women to be sober, to love their husbands, to love their children, To be discreet, chaste, keepers at home, good, obedient to their own husbands, that the word of God be not blasphemed.

Young men likewise exhort to be sober minded. In all things shewing thyself a pattern of good works: in doctrine shewing uncorruptness, gravity, sincerity, Sound speech, that cannot be condemned; that he that is of the contrary part may be ashamed, having no evil thing to say of you.

Exhort servants to be obedient unto their own masters, and to please them well in all things; not answering again;

Titus 2:1-9

EZEKIEL

1. THIS IS WHERE TO GO: EZEKIEL WAS TOLD WHERE TO GO.

And he said unto me, Son of man, GO, GET THEE UNTO THE HOUSE OF ISRAEL, and speak with my words unto them.

For thou art not sent to a people of a strange speech and of an hard language, but to the house of Israel; not to many people of a strange speech and of an hard language, whose words thou canst not understand. Surely, had I sent thee to them, they would have hearkened unto thee.

Ezekiel 3:4-6

And go, GET THEE TO THEM OF THE CAPTIVITY, unto the children of thy people, and speak unto them, and tell them, Thus saith the Lord God; whether they will hear, or whether they will forbear.

Ezekiel 3:11

2. THIS IS WHAT TO PREACH: EZEKIEL WAS TOLD WHAT TO PREACH.

Again he said unto me, prophesy upon these bones, and SAY UNTO THEM, O YE DRY BONES, HEAR THE WORD OF THE LORD.

Thus saith the Lord God unto these bones; behold, I will cause breath to enter into you, and ye shall live: and I will lay sinews upon you, and will bring up flesh upon you, and cover you with skin, and put breath in you, and ye shall live; and ye shall know that I am the Lord.

Ezekiel 37:4-6

3. EZEKIEL MADE FULL PROOF OF HIS MINISTRY.

So I prophesied as I was commanded: and as prophesied, there was a noise, and behold a shaking, and THE BONES CAME TOGETHER, bone to his bone. And when I beheld, lo, the sinews and the flesh came up upon them, and the skin covered them above: but there was no breath in them.

Ezekiel 37:7-8

So I prophesied as he commanded me, and THE BREATH CAME INTO THEM, and they lived, and stood up upon their feet, an exceeding great army.

Ezekiel 37:10

THE SEVENTY

1. THIS IS WHERE TO GO: THE SEVENTY SENT BY JESUS WERE TOLD WHERE TO GO.

After these things the Lord appointed other seventy also, and sent them two and two before his face INTO EVERY CITY AND PLACE, WHITHER HE HIMSELF WOULD COME.

Luke 10:1

2. THIS IS WHAT TO PREACH: THE SEVENTY SENT BY JESUS WERE TOLD WHAT TO PREACH.

Go your ways: behold, I send you forth as lambs among wolves. Carry neither purse, nor scrip, nor shoes: and salute no man by the way.

And into whatsoever house ye enter, FIRST SAY, PEACE BE TO THIS HOUSE. And if the son of peace be there, your peace shall rest upon it: if not, it shall turn to you again. And in the same house remain, eating and drinking such things as they give: for the labourer is worthy of his hire. Go not from house to house.

And into whatsoever city ye enter, and they receive you, eat such things as are set before you: and heal the sick that are therein, and SAY UNTO THEM, THE KINGDOM OF GOD IS COME NIGH UNTO YOU.

Luke 10:3-9

3. THE SEVENTY MADE FULL PROOF OF THEIR MINISTRY.

And the seventy returned again with joy, saying, Lord, EVEN THE DEVILS ARE SUBJECT UNTO US THROUGH THY NAME. And he said unto them, I beheld Satan as lightning fall from heaven.

Luke 10:17-18

THE APOSTLES

1. THIS IS WHERE TO GO: THE APOSTLES WERE TOLD WHERE TO GO.

And he said unto them, GO YE INTO ALL THE WORLD, and preach the gospel to every creature.

Mark 16:15

2. THIS IS WHAT TO PREACH: THE APOSTLES WERE TOLD WHAT TO PREACH.

And he said unto them, go ye into all the world, and PREACH THE GOSPEL to every creature.

Mark 16:15

3. THE APOSTLES MADE FULL PROOF OF THEIR MINISTRY.

And they went forth, and preached every where, the Lord working with them, and confirming the word WITH SIGNS FOLLOWING. Amen.

Mark 16:20

Howbeit MANY OF THEM WHICH HEARD THE WORD BELIEVED; and the number of the men was about FIVE THOUSAND.

Acts 4:4

PAUL

1. THIS IS WHERE TO GO: PAUL WAS TOLD WHERE TO GO.

Nevertheless, brethren, I have written the more boldly unto you in some sort, as putting you in mind, because of the grace that is given to me of God, THAT I SHOULD BE THE MINISTER OF JESUS CHRIST TO THE GENTILES, ministering the gospel of God, that the offering up of the Gentiles might be acceptable, being sanctified by the Holy Ghost.

Romans 15:15-16

2. THIS IS WHAT TO PREACH: PAUL WAS TOLD WHAT TO PREACH.

And I, brethren, when I came to you, came not with excellency of speech or of wisdom, declaring unto you the testimony of God. For I determined not to know any thing among you, save JESUS CHRIST, AND HIM CRUCIFIED. And I was with you in weakness, and in fear, and in much trembling.

AND MY SPEECH AND MY PREACHING WAS NOT WITH ENTICING WORDS OF MAN'S WISDOM, BUT IN DEMONSTRATION OF THE SPIRIT AND OF POWER:

Howbeit we speak wisdom among them that are perfect: yet not the wisdom of this world, nor of the princes of this world, that come to nought: But we speak the wisdom of God in a mystery, even the hidden wisdom, which God ordained before the world unto our glory:

1 Corinthians 2:1-4, 6-7

For I delivered unto you first of ALL THAT WHICH I ALSO RECEIVED, how that Christ died for our sins according to the scriptures;

1 Corinthians 15:3

3. PAUL MADE FULL PROOF OF HIS MINISTRY.

I have fought a good fight, I HAVE FINISHED MY COURSE, I HAVE KEPT THE FAITH: Henceforth there is laid up for me a crown of righteousness, which the Lord, the righteous judge, shall give me at that day: and not to me only, but unto all them also that love his appearing.

2 Timothy 4:7-8

CHAPTER 13

Fulfil Your Mission

I, even I, have spoken; yes, I have called him. I will bring him, and HE WILL SUCCEED IN HIS MISSION.

Isaiah 48:15

What It Means To Be on a Mission

God is a God of missions. He loves to call people and send them on missions. A reward awaits you when you are able to accomplish your mission.

To be on a mission is to be given a special assignment. Most people think to be on a mission is to travel somewhere to preach the Word of God. However, there are many missions in the Great Commission. Within the Great Commission are many possible jobs in God's vineyard.

Develop yourself in whatever mission you are given. Consider every assignment as something important. Most ministries do not start with preaching. Most of the ministry begins with serving. I want to share with you, seven different ways to fulfil your mission. Think about it in this way;

1. Fulfil your mission by doing your duties;

> JESUS KNEW THAT HIS MISSION WAS NOW FINISHED, and to fulfil Scripture he said, "I am thirsty."
>
> John 19:28 (NLT)

Jesus Christ is the ultimate person on the most profound mission of all time. He was given the duty of rescuing this lost and dying world from the arms of Satan. What a difficult task! Most people who have tried to change this world have failed. The world is a difficult place to work in. His duty was to shed His blood for mankind. His duty was not to build a dam, a school, a hospital or a university. His duty was to shed His blood. And He did just that! Can you carry out your mission? Can you give your life if that is what is required? Obedience will make you the most famous person on earth.

2. Fulfil your mission by doing your assignments.

Many times there is work to be done behind the scenes. If it is singing, playing instruments, serving, ensure that you complete whatever duty is given to you. Do not despise the duties that have been given to you. You may not know the importance of those duties.

Assignments speak of homework that you must do patiently and diligently. Failure to do your assignment makes you look silly when your work is called for. It is easy to see those who will never be promoted by the way they do their assignments.

3. Fulfil your mission by following your instructions.

> Samuel said, "Is it not true, though you were little in your own eyes, you were made the head of the tribes of Israel? And the Lord anointed you king over Israel, and THE LORD SENT YOU ON A MISSION, and said, "Go and utterly destroy the sinners, the Amalekites, and fight against them until they are exterminated." Why then did you not obey the voice of the Lord, but rushed upon the spoil and did what was evil in the sight of the Lord?"
>
> Then Saul said to Samuel, "I did obey the voice of the Lord, AND WENT ON THE MISSION ON WHICH THE LORD SENT ME, and have brought back Agag the king of Amalek, and have utterly destroyed the Amalekites.
>
> 1 Samuel 15:17-20 (NASB)

Saul was sent on a mission to kill and utterly destroy the Amalekites, including women and children. This mission was his undoing because he did not follow his instructions.

What are instructions? Instructions are clear orders issued to you. It is important to learn how to take instructions. Many people fail in their ministries because they never learn how to take instructions. In certain jobs you will be trained by an instructor. To fly a plane, you must be trained by an instructor. You will be told what to do and your opinion does not matter. In the military, you will be equally trained by instructors. Your ideas, your opinions and your methods are simply not needed or wanted. The difference between instructions and discussions is quite simple.

Instructions must be followed, no matter what. There are many people who are sent on a mission and simply do not carry out their instructions. These people do not end up well. In the military you will hear the instructors yelling at recruits, "If you do not follow my instructions, you will die!" That is exactly what happens to people. They die because they simply do not follow instructions.

Many people are unhappy in their marriages because they do not follow the instructions that are given to them. Many of the things to do in marriage do not make logical sense but they must be done. People who do not know how to follow instructions are doomed to fail. History proves that people who do not follow instructions soon lose the favour they have with higher authorities. God was quick to abandon Saul when He realized he would not obey instructions. There is no need for you to lose favour. Learn to mindlessly follow instructions when you receive them.

4. Fulfil your mission by carrying out an undertaking.

An undertaking is something you sign up for and agree to do. In order to fulfil your mission you must be able to stick to your word and do all the things you have agreed to. I once sent a missionary to a country far away on an island. Initially, he said God had told him to go on the mission. Two weeks after he arrived, he claimed that God had given him another calling to write books. He abandoned the mission and insisted on coming back home within a few weeks. We had invested a lot of money in sending this man to the mission field, only to bring him back a few weeks later at great cost. Such people do not keep to their word and are unreliable. You cannot work with people who do not keep to the things they say.

Watch out for unreliable people. They will sign agreements but it means nothing to them.

5. Fulfil your mission by carrying out an operation.

> And Barnabas and Saul returned from Jerusalem when they had FULFILLED THEIR MISSION, taking along with them John, who was also called Mark.
>
> Acts 12:25 (NASB)

Paul and Barnabas were on a mission to bring the gospel to Asia. This was no simple mission. It was a special operation.

An operation is a special mission involving a multiplicity of odd and unrelated jobs. Can you accept to do a series of odd jobs? Can you learn to do many unrelated things? You will never be used on a special operation if you cannot do unrelated jobs. Being able to do odd and unrelated jobs is key to becoming an important missionary.

To be successful on a mission field you have to learn how to pray, counsel, visit and interact with people. You will have to learn how to do administrative work, financial work, accounting work, construction work, architectural work, engineering work, management work and even political work. The reason why many people do not do well on the mission field is because they cannot or do not want to do the many unrelated things that are required of them. There are many people who feel their mission must involve only one kind of job. Maybe, all they want to do is to pray. Sometimes, people want to sit in an office and send emails. There are those who want to work on the field. Such a person cannot be sent on a special operation. The most valuable people are those who can follow instructions.

6. Fulfil your mission by taking up responsibilities.

> When Sarah, my master's wife, was very old, she gave birth to my master's son, and my master has given him everything he owns. And my master made me take an oath.

> He said, "Do not allow my son to marry one of these local Canaanite women. Go instead to my father's house, to my relatives, and find a wife there for my son."
>
> But I said to my master, "What if I can't find a young woman who is willing to go back with me?" He responded, "The Lord, in whose presence I have lived, will send his angel with you and will MAKE YOUR MISSION SUCCESSFUL. Yes, you must find a wife for my son from among my relatives, from my father's family. Then you will have fulfilled your obligation. But if you go to my relatives and they refuse to let her go with you, you will be free from my oath."
>
> "So today when I came to the spring, I prayed this prayer: 'O Lord, God of my master, Abraham, please give me success on this mission.'"
>
> Genesis 24:36-42 (NLT)

Abraham had to entrust a very important mission into the hands of his servant, Eliezar. Eliezar had to be very responsible to ensure that Abraham's lineage was preserved. Eliezar could just have chosen any girl he saw on the way and broken his master's trust. Why bother to go all the way to find Rebekah? Are there no pretty girls in the next town? There are times you can only send someone with a high sense of responsibility. A responsible person can be entrusted with people's lives.

There are jobs that are great responsibilities with momentous implications. Many people cannot do jobs that require a high level of responsibility. Responsibility is given to those who have a high sense of duty and will not let you down on something very important. Are you responsible?

Remember that jobs have different levels of importance. You can ask somebody to stand at the gate from morning till evening, opening and closing the gate as people come in. Such jobs do not have a high level of responsibility. There are higher duties like being a pilot. A little mistake by a pilot could kill four hundred people. The many little duties of a pilot must be carried out meticulously, otherwise his passengers can expect to die. Your sense of responsibility must be very high if you are a pilot.

Can God send you to nations where the lives of people will depend on your obedience? Or should God use you as an usher to greet people as they come in and out of the church. Greeting people as they come in and out of the church does not involve a high sense of responsibility. A failure to greet may not even be noticed. Decide to become someone who can be trusted with people's lives.

CHAPTER 14

Become A Good Missionary

As they ministered to the Lord, and fasted, the Holy Ghost said, Separate me Barnabas and Saul for the work whereunto I have called them. And when they had fasted and prayed, and laid their hands on them, they sent them away.

So they, being sent forth by the Holy Ghost, departed unto Seleucia; and from thence they sailed to Cyprus.

Acts 13:2-4

Become a good missionary and you will make full proof of your ministry! Becoming a good missionary will lead to the fulfilment of your ministry. Have a proper respect for the principles of being a good missionary. As you endeavour to become a good missionary, you will make full proof of your ministry!

Twelve Qualities of a Good Missionary

1. **If you say someone is a missionary, it means he is a good errand boy just like the twelve apostles.**

The disciples carried out the instructions of Jesus.

> When they were filled, HE SAID UNTO HIS DISCIPLES, GATHER UP THE FRAGMENTS that remain, that nothing be lost. Therefore they gathered them together, and filled twelve baskets with the fragments of the five barley loaves, which remained over and above unto them that had eaten.
>
> John 6:12-13

2. **If you say someone is a missionary, it means he is an ardent devotee.**

Paul devoted himself to the word of God because he was a good missionary.

> But when Silas and Timothy came down from Macedonia, Paul began DEVOTING HIMSELF COMPLETELY TO THE WORD, solemnly testifying to the Jews that Jesus was the Christ.
>
> Acts 18:5 (NASB)

3. **If you say someone is a missionary, it means he has become an admirer.**

Admiration is an important spiritual quality. Admiration is the sister of faith. When you believe in someone, you quickly become an admirer of the person. Unfortunately, some people do not grow in admiration of their leader. To be a good missionary you must become not only a believer, but an admirer.

Seeing it is a righteous thing with God to recompense tribulation to them that trouble you; And to you who are troubled rest with us, when the Lord Jesus shall be revealed from heaven with his mighty angels, In flaming fire taking vengeance on them that know not God, and that obey not the gospel of our Lord Jesus Christ:

> Who shall be punished with everlasting destruction from the presence of the Lord, and from the glory of his power; when he shall come to be glorified in his saints, and to be ADMIRED IN ALL THEM THAT BELIEVE (because our testimony among you was believed) in that day.
>
> 2 Thessalonians 1:6-10

4. If you say someone is a missionary it means he is a genuine fan, a backer, a supporter and a promoter.

A backer and a fan is a supporter of your cause. Joseph of Arimathaea was a supporter of Jesus Christ. When everyone supported the murder of Jesus Christ, Joseph of Arimathaea did not support it.

> And, behold, there was a man named Joseph, a counsellor; and he was a good man, and a just: (THE SAME HAD NOT CONSENTED TO THE COUNSEL AND DEED OF THEM;) he was of Arimathaea, a city of the Jews: who also himself waited for the kingdom of God. This man went unto Pilate, and begged the body of Jesus.
>
> Luke 23:50-52

5. If you say someone is a missionary, it means he is a real disciple.

Only a real disciple can be a good missionary. You will notice that it was the disciples that were sent on a mission to the whole world. It was not the managers or the bishops.

And when he had called unto him his twelve disciples, he gave them power against unclean spirits, to cast them out, and to heal all manner of sickness and all manner of disease. . . THESE TWELVE JESUS SENT FORTH, and commanded them, saying, Go not into the way of the Gentiles, and into any city of the Samaritans enter ye not:

Matthew 10:1, 5

And there was a certain disciple at Damascus, named Ananias; and to him said the Lord in a vision, Ananias. And he said, Behold, I am here, Lord. And the Lord said unto him, Arise, and go into the street which is called Straight, and enquire in the house of Judas for one called Saul, of Tarsus: for, behold, he prayeth.

Acts 9:10-11

6. **If you say someone is a missionary, it means he is a hard follower.**

And Jesus, walking by the sea of Galilee, saw two brethren, Simon called Peter, and Andrew his brother, casting a net into the sea: for they were fishers. And he saith unto them, FOLLOW ME, AND I WILL MAKE YOU FISHERS OF MEN. And they straightway left their nets, and followed him.

Matthew 4:18-20

7. **If you say someone is a missionary, it means he is a dependable messenger.**

Notice how the best and greatest missionaries of all time, the apostles, were messengers.

Now the first day of the feast of unleavened bread the disciples came to Jesus, saying unto him, Where wilt thou that we prepare for thee to eat the passover?

And he said, GO INTO THE CITY TO SUCH A MAN, AND SAY UNTO HIM, THE MASTER SAITH, My time is at hand; I will keep the passover at thy house with my disciples. And the disciples did as Jesus had appointed them; and they made ready the Passover.

Matthew 26:17-19

8. **If you say someone is a missionary, it means he is a radical propagandist and proselytizer and a radical converter of people.**

Then saith the woman of Samaria unto him, How is it that thou, being a Jew, askest drink of me, which am a woman of Samaria? For the Jews have no dealings with the Samaritans.

The woman then left her waterpot, and went her way into the city, and saith to the men, COME, SEE A MAN, WHICH TOLD ME ALL THINGS THAT EVER I DID: is not this the Christ?

John 4:9, 28-29

9. **If you say someone is a missionary, it means he is a good preacher and a systematic indoctrinator.**

Without the ability to indoctrinate and teach people, you will never be able to get them to follow you anywhere. This is why people who cannot get their wives to follow them to the mission field cannot be good missionaries. They are unable to indoctrinate even one person.

Whereunto I AM ORDAINED A PREACHER, and an apostle, (I speak the truth in Christ, and lie not;) A TEACHER of the Gentiles in faith and verity.

1 Timothy 2:7

10. If you say someone is a missionary, it means he is a powerful agent, an advocate and a go-between.

Ministers of the gospel have the ministry of reconciliation. They are sent to reconcile the world to God. We are to act as a go-between between God and man. We are God's agents on the ground. We are the ones He is trusting to bring about the reconciliation.

> And all things are of God, who hath reconciled us to himself by Jesus Christ, and hath given to us the MINISTRY OF RECONCILIATION;
>
> 2 Corinthians 5:18

11. If you say someone is a missionary, it means he is a faithful ambassador and a special envoy.

> Now then WE ARE AMBASSADORS FOR CHRIST, as though God did beseech you by us: we pray you in Christ's stead, be ye reconciled to God.
>
> 2 Corinthians 5:20

12. If you say someone is a missionary, it means he is a trustworthy carrier.

A missionary is a carrier of good tidings. He brings good news to the people and they rejoice because they have heard wonderful things about God.

> How then shall they call on him in whom they have not believed? and how shall they believe in him of whom they have not heard? and how shall they hear without a preacher? And how shall they preach, except they be sent? as it is written, How beautiful are the feet of them that preach the gospel of peace, and BRING GLAD TIDINGS OF GOOD THINGS!
>
> Romans 10:14-15

CHAPTER 15

Become God's Battle Axe

THOU ART MY BATTLE AXE AND WEAPONS OF WAR: for with thee will I break in pieces the nations, and with thee will I destroy kingdoms;

And with thee will I break in pieces the horse and his rider; and with thee will I break in pieces the chariot and his rider;

With thee also will I break in pieces man and woman; and with thee will I break in pieces old and young; and with thee will I break in pieces the young man and the maid;

I will also break in pieces with thee the shepherd and his flock; and with thee will I break in pieces the husbandman and his yoke of oxen; and with thee will I break in pieces captains and rulers.

Jeremiah 51:20-23

Become God's battle-axe and you will make full proof of your ministry! Becoming God's battle-axe is to walk in the supernatural path to the fulfilment of your ministry. Becoming God's battle-axe is becoming a weapon in the hands of God. Becoming a weapon in God's hands will cause you to make full proof of your ministry!

What Does It Mean to be God's Battle-Axe?

God wants you to be His battle-axe! God wants you to be His weapon of war! God wants to fight with you as His principal weapon. I once said to someone, "You are my secret weapon." This person had become a tool in my hand to help me accomplish great things. Read the Bible carefully and you will discover God's desire to use you as His secret weapon to defeat all works of darkness. Jesus Christ was manifested to destroy the works of the devil.

It is time to become a weapon in the hands of God. 'With you I will shatter nations and destroy many kingdoms.' With you He will shatter armies — destroying the horse and rider, the chariot and charioteer. With you He will shatter men and women, old people and children, young men and maidens. With you He will shatter shepherds and flocks, farmers and oxen, captains and officers. God will use you greatly to affect all types of people. That is what it means to be a weapon in the hands of God.

Today, we use missiles instead of axes and arrows. A missile is a more modern weapon. In today's language, Jeremiah 51 is telling you to become God's missile. There are many kinds of missiles in the world today. In the olden days, they had swords, axes, spears and knives. Spears and arrows were hand-propelled missiles of ancient times. Those were their weapons. In our day, modern weapons consist of bullets, rockets, short-range missiles, ballistic missiles and nuclear-powered rockets. God wants you to be His weapon in this modern era. Indeed, He wants you to be His missile that He can launch against a distant enemy. To be God's missile is to follow the instructions of Jeremiah and become a weapon in the hands of God.

What Does It Mean to be God's Missile?

1. **God's missile is a self-motivated person.** *A missile is a self-propelling device. A missile can travel for hundreds of miles without being prodded or guided to go in the right direction.* When you become God's missile, it means you are self-propelling and you do not need external input or supervision to make you move in the right direction. Many people need a whole lot of supervision, guidance, rebukes and correction before they move in the right direction or accomplish anything.

2. **God's missile is someone who can be sent to a far away location to accomplish great things.** *A missile is a weapon that can be thrown or fired at a target from a distance.* When you become God's missile, it means you can be thrown at a target from a distance. Perhaps, you are training in one country only for God to use you far away in another country. You are an internationally useful weapon. You may come from South Africa, but you may be used by God in Namibia. You may come from London but God will use you in Australia.

3. **God's missile is someone who will accomplish the mission.** *A missile is a weapon that is fired at a target from a far away location.* A missile may be fired from a submarine, a ship, a plane or from the ground. No matter where it is fired from, it hits the target and destroys it. There are many people who cannot be given a simple instruction. They simply will not obey commands. They will not catch the vision and will not run with it. You must be someone who can be programmed with a vision and a mission and will go forth and accomplish it.

4. **God's missile is someone who can be thrown into the frontline.** *A missile is a weapon that is designed to be thrown forwards.* Many people cannot be pushed into the frontline of ministry. The frontline of ministry is the mission field. Many people want to be in the ministry

but want stay at home where it is nice and safe. They want to sing in the choir and attend weddings. They do not want to go out there where it is dark and the voice of God is heard small. They do not want to go where the light is dim and few have dared venture. If you are God's missile, you can be launched into distant lands.

5. **God's missile is someone who can be directed from afar.** *A missile is a weapon that is fired at a target and may be directed by remote control.* There are many people who are good happy Christians and good Christian workers when they are around you. However when they are sent away, they are of no use because they do not communicate. Because they do not communicate, they cannot be directed, instructed or imparted to from afar. They become isolated and dangerous. God's missile is someone who can be directed from afar. Make sure you master the art of communication if you are to be an effective missile for God.

6. **God's missile is someone who can be sent to cause a great revival, awakening and stirring in a far away nation.** *A missile is a rocket with an exploding warhead or a nuclear bomb.* Indeed, a nuclear bomb will cause a great awakening among the people it is fired into. There will be no small commotion when the nuclear bomb hits its target. In the same way, when you are God's missile, you will cause a great stirring when you arrive at your destination. God will use you mightily and many thousands will be saved because you went.

7. **God's missile is someone who can move swiftly and suddenly.** *A missile is a rocket that moves through the air swiftly and suddenly.* Most effective missionaries and servants of God are people who move with high speed. Most failures move slowly! You will never fail! God has raised you up as His missile, His special weapon. God will use you on the mission field to raise up an army who will in turn go out and win more souls.

It is time to accept your role as God's weapon of war.

God has said clearly "You are my hammer and my *weapon of war.*" God will use you to smash godless nations!

God will use you to knock kingdoms to bits. God will use you to smash horse and rider;

God will use you to smash chariot and rider. God will use you to smash man and woman;

God will use you to smash the old man and the boy. God will use you to smash the young man and young woman; God will use you to smash shepherd and sheep. God will use you to smash farmer and yoked oxen, God will use you to smash governors and senators!

CHAPTER 16

Find God's Purpose

THE LORD HAS MADE EVERYTHING FOR ITS OWN PURPOSE, even the wicked for the day of evil.

Proverbs 16:4 (NASB)

Find God's purpose for your life and you will make full proof of your ministry! Finding God's purpose for your life is to begin the journey to the fulfilment of your ministry. Have a proper respect for seeking the purposes of God. Do not make assumptions! Do not be presumptuous! As you seek to find God's purpose for your life, you will make full proof of your ministry!

You can only fulfil your ministry by understanding the purposes of God. Purpose is the reason behind the things that are being done. God has a purpose for everything that He is doing. Seeking the mystery of His will is not enough. You must search out the purposes of God that are even more mysterious. It is necessary to know the purpose behind the will of God.

God has a purpose for you. Even when you are in the will of God, you must seek His purpose. Knowing the will of God is great, but knowing why the will of God is so, is even higher!

Wherefore be ye not unwise, but UNDERSTANDING what the will of the Lord is.

Ephesians 5:17

What are the unspoken purposes of God for your ministry? Why did God call you? Be wise and begin to understand the will of the Lord for you.

God is serious about His purpose

1. **Everything that has been made has its purpose.** Lay pastors, full time pastors, and missionaries have a purpose to fulfil. There is a reason for all the different sections of ministry that God has created.

THE LORD HAS MADE EVERYTHING FOR ITS OWN PURPOSE, even the wicked for the day of evil.

Proverbs 16:4 (NASB)

2. **God has a purpose and He has stretched out His hand to accomplish it.** Once God has purposed it, it will definitely come to pass.

THIS IS THE PURPOSE THAT IS PURPOSED upon the whole earth: and this is the hand that is stretched out upon all the nations.

Isaiah 14:26

3. **Who can frustrate or destroy the purpose of God?** Can Reverend X or Pastor Z destroy the purposes of God? Can the departure of someone or the disloyalty of another destroy the purposes of God? The answer is No!

For the LORD of hosts hath PURPOSED, and WHO SHALL DISANNUL it? and his hand is stretched out, and who shall turn it back?

Isaiah 14:27

4. **God's purposes will be established.** It is God's purpose that is going to be established on the earth. No one's ideas are going to be established. No matter how great you are, God's purpose is what is going to stand at the end of the day.

Declaring the end from the beginning and from ancient times things which have not been done, Saying, 'MY PURPOSE WILL BE ESTABLISHED, And I will accomplish all My good pleasure';

Isaiah 46:10 (NASB)

5. **God is looking for a man of His purpose.** God will go to great lengths to ensure that His purpose comes to pass. He will pull people from everywhere till He gets His work done.

Calling a bird of prey from the east, THE MAN OF MY PURPOSE FROM A FAR country. Truly I have spoken;

truly I will bring it to pass. I have planned it, surely I will do it.

Isaiah 46:11 (NASB)

6. **Jesus never wavered from His purpose.** Jesus always had God's purpose on His heart. God's purpose was to destroy the works of the devil through Jesus Christ. Jesus never deviated from this purpose till He left the earth.

He that committeth sin is of the devil; for the devil sinneth from the beginning. FOR THIS PURPOSE THE SON OF GOD WAS MANIFESTED, that he might destroy the works of the devil.

1 John 3:8

And when day came, He departed and went to a lonely place; and the multitudes were searching for Him, and came to Him, and tried to keep Him from going away from them.

But He said to them, "I MUST PREACH THE KINGDOM OF GOD TO THE OTHER CITIES ALSO, FOR I WAS SENT FOR THIS PURPOSE."

And He kept on preaching in the synagogues of Judea.

Luke 4:42-44 (NASB)

7. **Some people have purposed to fight against us and we must also purpose to fight against them in every possible way.**

After these things, and the establishment thereof, Sennacherib king of Assyria came, and entered into Judah, and encamped against the fenced cities, and thought to win them for himself.

And when Hezekiah saw that Sennacherib was come, AND THAT HE WAS PURPOSED TO FIGHT AGAINST JERUSALEM,

He took counsel with his princes and his mighty men to stop the waters of the fountains which were without the city: and they did help him.

2 Chronicles 32:1-3

8. **The purpose of God for you will end when your days on earth are past.** The purpose that God has for your life will end when your life is over. Make sure that you do the will of God and find out His purposes before then.

MY DAYS ARE PAST, my purposes are broken off, even the thoughts of my heart.

Job 17:11

9. **If things are going to work out, we must do everything according to God's purpose.** We are called according to His purpose.

And we know that all things work together for good to them that love God, to them who are the CALLED ACCORDING TO HIS PURPOSE.

Romans 8:28

CHAPTER 17

Walk in the Grace

Thou therefore, my son, be strong in the grace that is in Christ Jesus.

2 Timothy 2:1

Walk in the grace of God and you will make full proof of your ministry! Walking in the grace of God is to walk in the supernatural path that leads to the fulfilment of your ministry. It is time to understand the grace of God. It is time to walk in the grace of God. Have a proper respect for what the grace of God has done in your life. Have a proper respect for the grace of God and you will most definitely make full proof of your ministry!

This chapter is about the grace of God and your ministry. The ministry does not only work through the call of God, the will of God and the purposes of God. You will also need to flow in the grace of God. You will fulfil your ministry by flowing in the grace of God that is available for you. Grace means undeserved help, blessings and concessions. These concessions are things that God gives to surround the gift of God. It is the grace of God that makes certain things really work out in a beautiful way.

1. The grace of God determines how far your ministry will go.

The grace of God is why some pastors have larger churches whilst others have small churches. The grace of God is why some evangelists have larger crowds and some have smaller crowds. The grace of God is why some have more outstanding miracles and others have only minor miracles.

> **Be not thou therefore ashamed of the testimony of our Lord, nor of me his prisoner: but be thou partaker of the afflictions of the gospel according to the power of God; who hath saved us, and called us with an holy calling, not according to our works, but ACCORDING TO his own purpose and GRACE, which was given us in Christ Jesus before the world began,**
>
> **2 Timothy 1:8-9**

2. **The grace of God is what makes your gift available to many people.**

In the scripture below, you can see that it was the grace of God that brought salvation to many people. It is the grace of God that will bring your gift to many people. This is why some people have a lot of patronage for their ministry. This is why some people have many people reading their books, many people attending their churches and many people supporting them.

> **For THE GRACE OF GOD THAT BRINGETH SALVATION hath appeared to all men, teaching us that, denying ungodliness and worldly lusts, we should live soberly, righteously, and godly, in this present world;**
>
> **Titus 2:11-12**

3. **The grace of God causes much support to abound towards your ministry.**

> **And with great power gave the apostles witness of the resurrection of the Lord Jesus: and GREAT GRACE was upon them all. Neither was there any among them that lacked: for as many as were possessors of lands or houses sold them, and brought the prices of the things that were sold, and laid them down at the apostles feet: and distribution was made unto every man according as he had need.**
>
> **Acts 4:33-35**

The great grace upon the early church manifested as unity and financial provision. The disciples fulfilled their ministry according to the great support and unity they enjoyed.

You can fulfil your ministry according to the purpose of God. But you must also fulfil your ministry according to the grace of God. It manifests in blessings and help for the gifts of God that are in operation.

With every gift, there is an accompanying grace. The apostles were gifted men but the grace of God made their gift go even further. The grace of God made many people come together and support the good work that was being done in the early church.

4. **The grace of God can be seen by the great numbers that respond to the gift of God.**

Notice how great numbers responded to the ministry in Antioch. It was evident that the grace of God was working in a greater way in Antioch than anywhere else. When Barnabas arrived in Antioch, he saw the grace of God in action for himself. The grace of God is what causes your gift to be well received. This is why you must pray for the grace of God to work powerfully in your life and ministry. Grace refers to the collateral concessions that come along with the gift: kindness, blessings and riches.

> Now they which were scattered abroad upon the persecution that arose about Stephen travelled as far as Phenice, and Cyprus, and Antioch, preaching the word to none but unto the Jews only. And some of them were men of Cyprus and Cyrene, which, WHEN THEY WERE COME TO ANTIOCH, spake unto the Grecians, preaching the Lord Jesus. And the hand of the Lord was with them: and A GREAT NUMBER BELIEVED, AND TURNED UNTO THE LORD. Then tidings of these things came unto the ears of the church which was in Jerusalem: and they SENT FORTH BARNABAS, THAT HE SHOULD GO AS FAR AS ANTIOCH. Who, when he came, AND HAD SEEN THE GRACE OF GOD, was glad, and exhorted them all, that with purpose of heart they would cleave unto the Lord.
>
> For he was a good man, and full of the Holy Ghost and of faith: and much people was added unto the Lord.
>
> Acts 11:19-24

5. **You must be strong in the grace when you identify it.**

> **Thou therefore, my son, be strong in the grace that is in Christ Jesus.**
>
> **2 Timothy 2:1**

Paul asked Timothy to be strong in the grace of God. This meant that he should emphasize and major in things where he recognised the grace of God at work. Many people move away from the grace of God to what they feel is the ideal ministry. You must open your eyes and see what God has given you and what works for you. When the disciples saw that Antioch was experiencing the grace of God, they moved there and emphasized the ministry in that city. There was no point in holding on to Jerusalem as the headquarters of the ministry. The grace of God was working in Antioch and that is what they had to be strong in.

6. **God gives gifts according to the grace of God.**

Your gift is according to the grace and favour God has bestowed on you. Walk in the grace! Walk in the favour and your gift will affect even more people. My gift of pastoring affected more people when I realised that, God's grace was available for me to have many smaller branches, rather than one big church. The more I walked in that grace, the more I saw my gift working. Carefully analyse your ministry. Where and how is the grace of God working?

> **Having then GIFTS DIFFERING ACCORDING TO THE GRACE THAT IS GIVEN TO US, whether prophecy, let us prophesy according to the proportion of faith;**
>
> **Romans 12:6**

> **There is one body, and one Spirit, even as ye are called in one hope of your calling; one Lord, one faith, one baptism, one God and Father of all, who is above all, and through all, and in you all. BUT UNTO EVERY ONE OF US IS GIVEN GRACE ACCORDING TO THE MEASURE OF THE GIFT OF CHRIST.**
>
> **Ephesians 4:4-7**

CHAPTER 18

Follow the Visions

Whereupon, O king Agrippa, I was not disobedient unto the heavenly vision:

Acts 26:19

Follow the visions that God gives you and you will make full proof of your ministry! Following your visions is to walk in the supernatural path to the fulfilment of your ministry. Have a proper respect for visions. Have a proper respect for the visions God has mercifully granted you. As you flow with visions and dreams, you will make full proof of your ministry!

It is not possible to make full proof of your ministry without visions and dreams. Living in blindness and darkness will not help you in the ministry. Your eyes need to be opened to see visions that will guide you into the detailed steps of your ministry. An immediate effect of the presence of the Holy Spirit in your life is to see visions and have dreams.

> **And it shall come to pass in the last days, saith God, I will pour out of my Spirit upon all flesh: and your sons and your daughters shall prophesy, and your young men shall see visions, and your old men shall dream dreams: And on my servants and on my handmaidens I will pour out in those days of my Spirit; and they shall prophesy.**
>
> **Acts 2:17-18**

A great rebuke fell on the Laodicean church because it was blind. "Because thou sayest, I am rich, and increased with goods, and have need of nothing; and knowest not that thou art wretched, and miserable, and poor, AND BLIND, and naked: I counsel thee to buy of me gold tried in the fire, that thou mayest be rich; and white raiment, that thou mayest be clothed, and that the shame of thy nakedness do not appear; and ANOINT THINE EYES WITH EYESALVE, THAT THOU MAYEST SEE." (Revelation 3:17-18)

Obviously, God was not rebuking them for physical blindness. God is expecting you to deal with the blindness of your life and ministry by anointing your eyes so that you can see. Your eyes must be affected by the Holy Spirit! You must be influenced by the visions and dreams God gives you.

The Holy Spirit's effect on your life is to make you prophecy and to make you see visions. As you serve the Lord, your eyes will be opened.

May the Lord anoint your eyes with eye salve, so that you may see! Your eyes must open up and begin to see what the Lord sees. Without serious visions, you cannot fulfil your ministry. Visions come along the way to make things clear.

1. Visions are God's way of speaking to His anointed.

Then THOU SPAKEST IN VISION TO THY HOLY ONE, and saidst, I have laid help upon one that is mighty; I have exalted one chosen out of the people.

Psalm 89:19

Anointed and holy people are spoken to through visions and dreams. "*Thou spakest in a vision to Thy holy one*"! These are the words of David! These are words he spoke describing a vision he had received from God. He declared that God had spoken to him through visions and dreams. I remember an encounter I had with a little known man of God. I did not know much about him or his ministry. He was invited to speak at a dinner I was attending. When he spoke, I noticed something. He spoke of a vision he had had, in which God told him to leave his country and go to another country to establish a church. As he described the vision, I realised that he was a very anointed man of God. I did not know much about him, but I took note of him. A couple of years later, I saw him on television speaking to a massive church. Then I remembered that this was the man I had taken note of because of his visions. The visions a person may have will mark him out for the ministry.

2. Visions are God's way of speaking to His anointed men of understanding.

And he sought God in the days of Zechariah, who had UNDERSTANDING IN THE VISIONS OF GOD: and as long as he sought the Lord, God made him to prosper.

2 Chronicles 26:5

Zechariah was well known for his understanding of the visions of God. A person can have many dreams and visions and not understand anything he sees. It is important to see and understand the visions that God shows you. I remember a young man who called me and told me a vision that he had. In the vision, he saw himself caught up in a tree by his hair. As he narrated this vision to me, I wondered to myself, "What a vision, this is Absalom!"

Then I asked him, "What do you think this vision means?"

He said, "I think it means that a lot of people are jealous me and are trying to pull me back. When I am moving forward, they are grabbing me and preventing me from going ahead."

I was amazed that the pastor was giving this interpretation to his dream. The only thing that came to my mind was Absalom. It is only Absalom whose hair was caught in the branches of a tree. This young man was, however, convinced that the vision was a revelation of the jealous people in his life. A few weeks later, a spirit of rebellion overtook this brother and he behaved exactly like Absalom. He broke away from his spiritual father's house and attacked his own spiritual home. It is only an Absalom who attacks his own father. He manifested exactly what his dream was warning him about, but he had no understanding of his visions.

3. Visions are God's way of speaking to His anointed in their sleep.

> In thoughts from the VISIONS OF THE NIGHT, when deep sleep falleth on men,
>
> Job 4:13

Every night, an anointed person has an opportunity to hear from God. Through the visions of the night, God can and does speak to His servants. Indeed, if you are sensitive enough, you will even hear the Spirit ask you to go to bed so He can speak to you. One man of God heard the Holy Spirit telling him, "Go to bed. I need to speak to you." It seems that God can speak to us more easily when we are asleep.

Perhaps, the mind is quieter when we are asleep and He can introduce His thoughts into our heads. There are many guidelines to seeing visions. The Bible is quite clear that when you are experiencing something in your life you also dream about it. This makes it easy for you to discard many of the dreams that come to you through the multitude of business. Hungry people dream about food and thirsty people dream about drink. That is a simple formula to guide you in the ministry of dreams. Do not be moved by the visions and dreams you generate out of your needs and desires. Wait on the Lord and He will speak to you through genuine dreams and visions.

> It shall even be as when AN HUNGRY MAN DREAMETH, AND, BEHOLD, HE EATETH; but he awaketh, and his soul is empty:
> or as when A THIRSTY MAN DREAMETH, AND, BEHOLD, HE DRINKETH; but he awaketh, and, behold, he is faint, and his soul hath appetite: so shall the multitude of all the nations be, that fight against mount Zion.
>
> Isaiah 29:8

4. Visions are God's way of speaking to His anointed whilst they are awake.

> He hath said, which heard the words of God, which saw the vision of the Almighty, FALLING INTO A TRANCE, BUT HAVING HIS EYES OPEN: …
> He hath said, which heard the words of God, and knew the knowledge of the most High, which saw the vision of the Almighty, FALLING INTO A TRANCE, BUT HAVING HIS EYES OPEN:
>
> Numbers 24:4, 16

A trance is an experience you can have whilst you are awake. Your eyes are open but you have an experience that is so spiritual and so real. God speaks to His anointed through trances. Pray that you may fall into a trance. Do not be spooky about trances. When people speak of trances you immediately think of fortune-tellers, palm readers and witch doctors. However, trances are valid spiritual experiences from God. Apostle Peter fell into a trance when he was waiting for his dinner. He saw something unusual and this trance became the guiding post for the gospel to go to the Gentile world.

> On the morrow, as they went on their journey, and drew nigh unto the city, Peter went up upon the housetop to pray about the sixth hour: And he became very hungry, and would have eaten: but while they made ready, HE FELL INTO A TRANCE, And saw heaven opened, and a certain vessel descending unto him, as it had been a great sheet knit at the four corners, and let down to the earth:
>
> Acts 10:9-11

5. **Visions are God's way of assuring His anointed of His presence.**

> **And the child Samuel ministered unto the Lord before Eli. And the word of the Lord was precious in those days; THERE WAS NO OPEN VISION.**
>
> **1 Samuel 3:1**

The absence of visions and dreams is almost always linked to the absence of God's presence. In the days when Samuel was a child, there were no visions in Israel. Eli was the prophet of the day and he had fallen out of favour with God. Actually, God was getting ready to pour His judgment onto Eli. The absence of visions was the big sign that God's presence had departed from Israel. This is one of the main reasons why you must desire to have visions and dreams. The more dreams and visions you have, the more revelation you have. The more dreams and visions you have, the more of God's presence you have. The more dreams and visions you have, the closer you are to God.

The more dreams and visions you have, the more the Holy Spirit is with you.

6. Visions are God's way of preventing destruction.

WHERE THERE IS NO VISION, THE PEOPLE PERISH: but he that keepeth the law, happy is he.

Proverbs 29:18

Where there is no vision, there is destruction. People perish because of the lack of vision and direction. God wants you to have visions so that you have direction for your life and ministry. Visions are very important for your life and ministry. When I asked the Lord what would make me more fruitful, He showed me a vision of a hand holding a book. The vision of a book served to guide me in ministry. At a point you have many options and many different things you can do. Which one should you do? What is right for you to do? Visions and dreams are what you need to guide you into the next phase of ministry.

7. Visions are God's way of blessing your ministry with supernatural achievements.

The hand of the Lord was upon me, and carried me out in the spirit of the Lord, and set me down in the midst of the valley which was full of bones, And caused me to pass by them round about: and, behold, there were very many in the open valley; and, lo, they were very dry. And he said unto me, Son of man, can these bones live? And I answered, O Lord God, thou knowest. Again he said unto me, Prophesy upon these bones, and say unto them, O ye dry bones, hear the word of the Lord.

Ezekiel 37:1-4

Ezekiel had a vision from God. In this vision, he saw a valley of dry bones. In the vision, God asked him if the dry bones could possibly live again. He was asked to prophesy to the dry bones and to his amazement the valley of dry bones became a valley of living human beings. This impossible feat happened in Ezekiel's visions. God was showing him how He was going to use him to do supernatural, impossible, fantastic, amazing and wonderful things. Pray for God to show you the supernatural future of your ministry.

One day, early in my evangelistic ministry, I had a vision of myself climbing onto a stage for a crusade. Unfortunately, I met a mad man on the stairs who simply would not let me climb up the stairs. He fought with me to prevent me from going on the stage. At a point in the fight, I pushed him to the side and took a peep at the crowd. I was amazed at the fantastic sea of people that were waiting to hear me preach. The Holy Spirit whispered to me, "I have large crowds waiting to hear you preach." You must overcome the hindrances, obstacles and wicked demons that are fighting to keep you from seeing the glorious crowds of souls.

Through the visions of God, I was able to see the future and the kind of evangelistic ministry God had planned for me.

CHAPTER 19

Use Your Gift

For the kingdom of heaven is as a man travelling into a far country, who called his own servants, and delivered unto them his goods.

And unto one he gave five talents, to another two, and to another one; to every man according to his several ability; and straightway took his journey. THEN HE THAT HAD RECEIVED THE FIVE TALENTS WENT AND TRADED with the same, and made them other five talents. And likewise he that had received two, he also gained other two.

But he that had received one went and digged in the earth, and hid his lord's money.

Matthew 25:14-18

Use your gift and you will make full proof of your ministry! Using your gift is to start the journey to the fulfilment of your ministry. Have a proper respect for the small gift you have received. As you use the gift of God, you will find yourself making full proof of your ministry!

1. **The gift of God is your special ability that establishes you.**

For I long to see you, that I may impart unto you some spiritual gift, to the end YE MAY BE ESTABLISHED;

Romans 1:11

A gift is an ability! You know you have a gift when you are able to do something easily which others are unable to do. You must develop and use the gift God has given you. To be called by God is to receive a gift from God. This gift is a natural talent freely given to you by God. To be called by God is to be given a natural capacity for certain things.

This is why gifted people seem to do certain things effortlessly. If you are called to pastor a church, you will have the gift of effortlessly looking after troublesome people for many years. If you are called to evangelize you will have the gift of loving the poor masses that have nothing to give in return. If you have the gift of singing you will sing effortlessly whilst others struggle to even find the key. The Hebrew word for gift is *mattan*, which means a present. When you have a gift, it means God has given you a present.

2. **The gift of God is your special ability that creates an audience.**

A man's gift MAKETH ROOM for him, and bringeth him before great men.

Proverbs 18:16

It is the gift of God that causes you to stand before different audiences. If you continue to use the gift God has given you, you will find yourself standing before great men and great audiences. You cannot fulfil your ministry without the gift of God. A gift is what expands your ministry and brings you before great men. God has a gift for everyone who has yielded himself to the mysterious will of God. The gift of God lifts up your ministry into a wider, larger realm.

3. **The gift of God is your special ability that responds to your desires.**

Follow after charity, and desire spiritual gifts, but rather that ye may prophesy.

1 Corinthians 14:1

The unique characteristic about the gift of God is that it responds to desire. The more you desire the gift the more you receive! When you stand before a congregation that is filled with desire, interest, anticipation and excitement, the gift of God will flow naturally. Desire is the master key to receiving the gift of God. The desire for the gift is the key to any spiritual infilling. Blessed are they that thirst, for they shall be filled. Receiving an infilling of the gift of God is given to those who desire it and those who are thirsty.

It is difficult to give water to someone who is not thirsty! Whenever people have to drink water for medical reasons, they really struggle to drink if they are not thirsty. For example, I have seen people struggle to drink water in the hospital just before an exam that requires a full bladder, simply because they were not thirsty. How difficult it is to drink water when you are not thirsty! How difficult it is for people to receive gifts that they do not desire!

It is those who ask, who receive. It is those who seek that find! The door is opened only to those who knock. Your desire for something is greatly increased when you see it in action and are filled with admiration. I have never nurtured any secret desire to be a star singer. But I have had great admiration for preachers and I have nurtured secret desires to become a preacher. Anyone who walks in a gift has nurtured desires for the gift.

4. **The gift of God is your special ability that you may be neglecting.**

Neglect not the gift that is in thee, which was given thee by prophecy, with the laying on of the hands of the presbytery.

1 Timothy 4:14

Sometimes, people without gifts do better than people with gifts. This is because many gifted people neglect their gifts. There are singers who neglect their special ability to sing. There are musicians who neglect their special ability to play music. There are preachers and teachers who neglect their special ability to teach. You would think that people would naturally rise up and use their gifts. But the exact opposite is true. Most people neglect their gifts. I have marvelled at gifted musicians who neglect their God-given gift of a musical ear.

5. **The gift of God is your special ability that you may be ignorant about.**

Now concerning spiritual gifts, brethren, I would not have you ignorant.....

1 Corinthians 12:1

It is easy to be ignorant about spiritual gifts. This is why Paul bothered to teach about spiritual gifts.

Sometimes it takes an outsider to notice the gift of God in you. When someone notices the gift of God, you must pay attention to what he says. He may be the person God is using to point out your gift. A gift is a special ability that is so natural that it does not even seem supernatural or spiritual. This is why it sometimes takes an outsider to notice that you are gifted.

6. **The gift of God is your special ability that makes you very different from others.**

Having then GIFTS DIFFERING according to the grace that is given to us, whether prophecy, let us prophesy according to the proportion of faith;

Romans 12:6

The gifts of God are so different that it is a common thing for people to look at others and desire their gifts. Your gift makes you very different from others. You will find disorganized people who are gifted singers wishing they were organised administrators. You will find organised administrators wishing they had some grace to be able to stand on stage. You would find some preachers wishing they could sing. You would also find people with the gift of teaching, wishing they had the gift of healing. It is important to recognize that there are different types of gifts in the body. The great variety allows many things to be accomplished in the house of the Lord.

7. **The gift of God is your special ability that must be stirred up.**

Wherefore I put thee in remembrance that thou STIR UP THE GIFT OF GOD, which is in thee by the putting on of my hands.

2 Timothy 1:6

It is time to stir up the gift of God. Focus on your special ability. Give yourself to it! Become better at doing what you are good at doing. Do not let other people's gifts confuse you. You are gifted with a different gift and you need to stir it up. People who stir up the gift of God are often called hard diligent workers. Indeed, it is diligence, persistence and hard work that stir up the gift of God. When you come close to someone who has walked in the stirrings of his gift, you will often wonder whether he is gifted or just a hard worker.

CHAPTER 20

Stand in Your Office

And let these also first be proved; then let them use the OFFICE OF A DEACON, being found blameless…. For they that have used the OFFICE OF A DEACON well purchase to themselves a good degree, and great boldness in the faith which is in Christ Jesus.

1 Timothy 3:10, 13

Stand in your office and you will make full proof of your ministry! Standing in your office is to walk in the path that leads to the fulfilment of your ministry. Have a proper respect for the office. Do not only respect secular offices. As you respect your spiritual office, you will begin to make full proof of your ministry!

To be put in an office by the Lord is to be lifted into the highest ranks of ministry. What greater privilege can you have than to be given an office by the Lord? A whole office!

How to Know You Are in an Office of Ministry

a. Your ministry has developed into an office when you command authority.

b. Your ministry has developed into an office when you need help ministers to work for you.

c. Your ministry has developed into an office when you have a building, an office and staff.

d. Your ministry has developed into an office when you are in full-time ministry.

e. Your ministry has developed into an office when you have employees that work for you in the ministry.

1. Every ministry can become an office.

For as we have many members in one body, and all members have not THE SAME OFFICE:

Romans 12:4

You can fulfil your ministry by functioning in the office that God sets you in. Your ministry can develop until it becomes an office. When you have an office and you use it well, you purchase for yourself a great boldness towards God. When your ministry gets to a place where it works through and by helpers, you have entered an office. Your gift has grown into an office.

2. An office in ministry indicates a high rank.

And let these also first be proved; then let them use the office of a deacon, being found blameless…. For they that have used the OFFICE of a deacon well purchase to themselves a GOOD DEGREE, and GREAT BOLDNESS in the faith which is in Christ Jesus.

1 Timothy 3:10, 13

If you can work well through and with people (if they use the office well) you can earn a good degree. You must learn to work through and with people. You must come to the point where you are comfortable to have others shine.

3. Magnify the office God has given you.

For I speak to you Gentiles, inasmuch as I am the apostle of the Gentiles, I MAGNIFY MINE OFFICE:

Romans 11:13

It is important to make your ministry work important. Many people made fun of me when I spoke of the importance of shepherding. They mocked me and called my members names. The shepherd's office is a very important office. Jesus said the sheep are scattered because there is no shepherd. The sheep are not scattered because there is no prophet. A shepherd's office is very important. The art of shepherding can be developed until it evolves into an office.

This is why Paul magnified his office. If you do not magnify your office, Satan will continuously insult and denigrate your important work. When you begin to work with helpers you have begun to function in an office. When you work alone you are functioning as a solo ministry.

4. Every kind of ministry can be magnified until it becomes an office.

Whenever a ministry or a gift is taken seriously, it develops into an office. A priest can develop his ministry into a mighty office. A deacon can develop his ministry into an office. A singer can develop his ministry into an office. Helpers can develop their ministries into offices. Treasurers can develop their money-counting jobs into a full-fledged office. The scriptures below show us that all these little functions can become real offices. On the other hand, they can all remain as little odd jobs that people do in the house of God. Even the pastor can refuse to develop his ministry.

Many pastors have undeveloped ministries and therefore they are not needed on a full-time basis. Many pastors have undeveloped ministries and therefore do not need to have helpers or full-time employees working with them. In such cases, they do the ministry of a priest, but have not developed a priest's office.

The scriptures below show us the wonderful examples of many odd jobs that developed into full-fledged offices. It is time for you to develop your ministry into a full-fledged office. Today, I am still amazed at the number of people that have to be employed in the priest's office. I started out as a shepherd and a priest interceding for a few students. This little ministry of shepherding developed from caring for a handful of children in a slum, into an international shepherding office.

a. The priest's office.

> And this is the thing that thou shalt do unto them to hallow them, to minister unto me in THE PRIEST'S OFFICE: Take one young bullock, and two rams without blemish, and unleavened bread, and cakes unleavened tempered with oil, and wafers unleavened anointed with oil: of wheaten flour shalt thou make them.
>
> Exodus 29:1-2

b. The deacon's office.

> For they that have used THE OFFICE OF A DEACON well purchase to themselves a good degree, and great boldness in the faith which is in Christ Jesus.
>
> 1 Timothy 3:13

c. The helper's office.

> Because THEIR OFFICE WAS TO WAIT ON THE SONS OF AARON for the service of the house of the Lord, in the courts, and in the chambers, and in the purifying of all holy things, and the work of the service of the house of God;
>
> 1 Chronicles 23:28

d. The porter's office.

> And Zechariah the son of Meshelemiah was PORTER OF THE DOOR of the tabernacle of the congregation. All these which were chosen to be porters in the gates were two hundred and twelve. These were reckoned by their genealogy in their villages, whom David and SAMUEL THE SEER DID ORDAIN IN THEIR SET OFFICE.
>
> 1 Chronicles 9:21-22

e. The singer's office.

> And these are they whom David set over the service of song in the house of the Lord, after that the ark had rest. And THEY MINISTERED BEFORE THE DWELLING PLACE OF THE TABERNACLE OF THE CONGREGATION WITH SINGING, until Solomon had built the house of the Lord in Jerusalem: and then they WAITED ON THEIR OFFICE according to their order.
>
> 1 Chronicles 6:31-32

f. The treasurer's office.

> And I MADE TREASURERS over the treasuries, Shelemiah the priest, and Zadok the scribe, and of the Levites, Pedaiah: and next to them was Hanan the son of Zaccur, the son of Mattaniah: for they were counted faithful, and THEIR OFFICE WAS TO DISTRIBUTE unto their brethren.
>
> Nehemiah 13:13

CHAPTER 21

Move Through the Four Phases

For IN HIM WE LIVE, AND MOVE, and have our being; as certain also of your own poets have said, for we are also his offspring.

Acts 17:28

When you go through the four phases of your ministry, you will have made full proof of your ministry! Going through the four different phases of your ministry is to walk in the supernatural path to the fulfilment of your ministry. Have a deep understanding of the four phases of your ministry. Believe that you must pass through all the four different phases and you will definitely make full proof of your ministry!

To enter into your ministry is to enter the *first* phase of ministry. To persist in the ministry is to move through the *four* different phases of ministry.

To keep moving through the four phases of ministry you need to continually walk by faith. To keep moving through the four phases of ministry you need to constantly walk in humility. To keep moving through the four phases of ministry you need to continue making sacrifices to the Lord.

Anyone who stops walking by faith, stops going through the four phases of ministry. The door to the next phase of your ministry is a short humble door. Once you are no longer humble, you stop being able to enter the humble doors to the next phase of your ministry. To stay on at the same level in your ministry does not require much change from you. But to move on to the next phase of ministry will require more sacrifices from you.

When people are in ministry for some time, they feel they have 'arrived' so they do not try to move on. It is important to move on! It is important to keep moving! The Spirit is moving! The Spirit is always moving! In Him we move!

Once you are in Him, you are expected to move, because 'in Him' we move.

There is a lot of evidence to show that there are four phases to life and ministry. The seasons of the year reveal the four phases of our lives in one year. The first Psalm reveals that our lives work by seasons. The existence of the early and the latter rains also prove that there are four clear seasons. The season of the first rain, the season after the first rain, the season of the latter rain and the season after the latter rain, which is the harvest season.

However, the best example of the four phases of ministry is found in the ministry of Jesus Christ Himself.

1. Your ministry has four phases because life on earth has four phases.

Summer, Winter, Spring and Autumn are the four seasons in a year. It seems that God has created life to work out in four seasons. "While the earth remaineth, seedtime and harvest, and cold and heat, and summer and winter, and day and night shall not cease" (Genesis 8:22). Notice how the blessed man will bring forth fruit not all the time, but in his season.

> Blessed is the man that walketh not in the counsel of the ungodly, nor standeth in the way of sinners, nor sitteth in the seat of the scornful
>
> But his delight is in the law of the Lord; and in his law doth he meditate day and night.
>
> And he shall be like a tree planted by the rivers of water, THAT BRINGETH FORTH HIS FRUIT IN HIS SEASON; his leaf also shall not wither; and whatsoever he doeth shall prosper.
>
> Psalm 1:1-3

2. Your ministry has four phases because God comes to you as the latter rain and the former rain.

> Then shall we know, if we follow on to know the Lord: his going forth is prepared as the morning; and HE SHALL COME UNTO US AS THE RAIN, as the latter and former rain unto the earth.
>
> Hosea 6:3

God will pour out His Spirit in seasons. God does not do the same thing every day. God will come to you like the rain does.

He will come like the early rain and He will also come like the latter rain. This reality defines life into four seasons.

When God comes to you as the rain, your ministry changes and flourishes.

The first phase: There is a season where His relationship with you is like the pouring of the early rain. This early rain waters the seeds you have sown and causes the initial budding in the fields. He anoints you, He uses you and He blesses you. This former rain is well known to start you off in the ministry and bring you out of obscurity.

The second phase: Then there seems to be a season where He is not blessing you as much. This is a quiet season! This quiet season may last for a long time with things remaining collectively calm. In this season you are expected to grow quietly and humbly, developing the virtues of faithfulness, endurance and persistence.

The third phase: At a point, the rain begins to fall again. That is the latter rain! This latter rain brings the crops to maturity in readiness for harvest. In this season of your life you receive a booster and everything seems to be much bigger.

The fourth phase: In the fourth phase you are reaping the harvest in your ministry. Everything you have sown comes into maturity. It is harvest time! The latter rain is come and gone. In this fourth phase, you are preparing others to take over your 'room' in ministry.

3. **Your ministry has four phases because Jesus had four phases in His ministry.**

The first phase: Synagogues. The first phase of Jesus' ministry was His ministry in the synagogues. Jesus went to many towns and preached in the synagogues everywhere. Note how He moved into the synagogues as soon as He came back from the temptation in the wilderness. Note how he continued moving through the synagogues in the whole of Galilee. Perhaps the first phase of your ministry is to preach in churches. Perhaps the next phase of your ministry may not be within the church but outside the church.

And Jesus returned in the power of the Spirit into Galilee: and there went out a fame of him through all the region round about. And he taught in their synagogues, being glorified of all.

And he came to Nazareth, where he had been brought up: and, as his custom was, HE WENT INTO THE SYNAGOGUE on the sabbath day, and stood up for to read.

Luke 4:14-16

The second phase: Outside the Synagogues. The second phase of Jesus' ministry was His ministry outside the synagogues. He famously preached the beatitudes on a mountain and not in any synagogue. He also preached to thousands by the lakeside and by the sea of Tiberias. He ministered to thousands of people in desert places. Perhaps the next phase of your ministry is to be found in unconventional locations, ministering the Word of God.

And seeing the multitudes, he went up into a MOUNTAIN: and when he was set, his disciples came unto him:

Matthew 5:1

And it came to pass, that, as the people pressed upon him to hear the word of God, HE STOOD BY THE LAKE of Gennesaret,

Luke 5:1

And the apostles, when they were returned, told him all that they had done. And he took them, and went aside privately into A DESERT PLACE belonging to the city called Bethsaida. And the people, when they knew it, followed him: and he received them, and spake unto them of the kingdom of God, and healed them that had need of healing.

Luke 9:10-11

The third phase: Disciples. The third phase of Jesus' ministry was His ministry to the disciples. The book of John reveals that there was a time when Jesus Christ withdrew Himself from the larger public gatherings. We see that He then restricted Himself to His disciples. Most of the book of John is dedicated to this phase of private ministry.

From that time many of his disciples went back, and walked no more with him. Then said Jesus unto the twelve, Will ye also go away?

Then Simon Peter answered him, Lord, to whom shall we go? thou hast the words of eternal life.

And we believe and are sure that thou art that Christ, the Son of the living God.

Jesus answered them, Have not I chosen you twelve, and one of you is a devil?

He spake of Judas Iscariot the son of Simon: for he it was that should betray him, being one of the twelve.

John 6:66-71

Jesus therefore walked no more openly among the Jews; but went thence unto a country near to the wilderness, into a city called Ephraim, and there continued with his disciples.

John 11:54

The fourth phase: The cross. The fourth phase of Jesus' ministry was His journey to the cross. Going to the cross and giving Himself up to shed His blood was the paramount purpose for Jesus Christ in the fourth phase of His ministry.

First of all, it was preaching in established places of worship called synagogues. Second, He was preaching in larger unconventional locations. Thirdly, His ministry was confined to the disciples and finally His focus was the cross.

> And it came to pass, when the time was come that he should be received up, he steadfastly set his face to go to Jerusalem,
>
> Luke 9:51

4. Your ministry has four phases because Jesus had four phases in four different locations.

a. The first phase: Bethlehem.

The first phase of Jesus' ministry was in the first location of Bethlehem. Jesus was born in Bethlehem. This is where it all started! Starting your ministry is a most difficult endeavour. Starting your ministry is very different from continuing in an established ministry. To start something involves a great step of faith and a great step of humility.

> Now when JESUS WAS BORN IN BETHLEHEM of Judaea in the days of Herod the king, behold, there came wise men from the east to Jerusalem,
>
> Matthew 2:1

b. The second phase: Nazareth.

The second phase of Jesus' ministry was in the second location of Nazareth, the place of spiritual development. Nazareth was a quiet time for Jesus. Very little is known about His life and ministry in Nazareth. We never hear of Jesus preaching and we never hear of Him doing miracles. But we do hear of Him in the synagogues, listening and asking questions. We do hear of Him increasing in wisdom, in stature and in favour with God and man. During this second phase of ministry, Jesus was constantly studying, learning and receiving the wisdom of God. There is a phase of your ministry where you must give yourself more to studying, learning and receiving, rather than to giving out to others.

> And it came to pass, that after three days they found him in the temple, sitting in the midst of the doctors, both hearing them, and asking them questions. And all that heard him were astonished at his understanding and answers.
>
> And when they saw him, they were amazed: and his mother said unto him, Son, why hast thou thus dealt with us? behold, thy father and I have sought thee sorrowing. And he said unto them, How is it that ye sought me? wist ye not that I must be about my Father's business?
>
> And they understood not the saying which he spake unto them. And he went down with them, and came to NAZARETH, and was subject unto them: but his mother kept all these sayings in her heart. And Jesus increased in wisdom and stature, and in favour with God and man.
>
> Luke 2:46-52

> And it came to pass in those days, that Jesus came from NAZARETH of Galilee, and was baptized of John in Jordan.
>
> Mark 1:9

c. The third phase: Galilee.

The third phase of Jesus' ministry was in the third location of Galilee. Jesus Christ did many great things in Galilee. He had to move a few hundred kilometres away from Bethlehem, so that He would be well received. The villages and towns along the lakeside were extremely happy to receive the miracle worker. During this third phase of His ministry, Jesus performed most of the famous miracles that He was known for. As you can see, He did not perform these miracles everywhere nor in every phase of His ministry. It was during the Galilee phase of ministry that these things took place. Chorazin, Bethsaida and Capernaum were the main cities along the lake of Galilee, and this is where most of Jesus' miracle ministry took place.

> And JESUS RETURNED IN THE POWER OF THE SPIRIT INTO GALILEE: and there went out a fame of

him through all the region round about. And he taught in their synagogues, being glorified of all.

Luke 4:14-15

Then began he to upbraid the cities wherein most of his mighty works were done, because they repented not:

Woe unto thee, CHORAZIN! Woe unto thee, BETHSAIDA! For if the mighty works, where done in you, had been done in Tyre and Sidon, they would have repented long ago in sackcloth and ashes.

But I say unto you, it shall be more tolerable for Tyre and Sidon at the day of judgment, than for you.

And thou, CAPERNAUM, which art exalted unto heaven, shalt be brought down to hell: for if the mighty works, which have been done in thee, had been done in Sodom, it would have remained until this day.

But I say unto you, That it shall be more tolerable for the land of Sodom in the day of judgment, than for you.

Matthew 11:20-24

Now when Jesus had heard that John was cast into prison, he departed into Galilee; And leaving Nazareth, he came and dwelt in CAPERNAUM, which is upon the sea coast, in the borders of Zabulon and Nephthalim:

That it might be fulfilled which was spoken by Esaias the prophet, saying, The land of Zabulon, and the land of Nephthalim, by the way of the sea, beyond Jordan, Galilee of the Gentiles; The people which sat in darkness saw great light; and to them which sat in the region and shadow of death light is sprung up.

Matthew 4:12-16

d. The fourth phase: Jerusalem.

The fourth phase of Jesus' ministry was in the fourth location of Jerusalem. It was in Jerusalem that He was crucified. It was in Jerusalem that he shed His blood for the whole world. It is in Jerusalem that a huge church stands to commemorate the place where Jesus died on the cross for the whole world. Jesus accomplished the greatest harvest in Jerusalem.

> And it came to pass, when the time was come that he should be received up, he steadfastly SET HIS FACE TO GO TO JERUSALEM,
>
> Luke 9:51

> And when he had thus spoken, he went before, ASCENDING UP TO JERUSALEM.
>
> And it came to pass, when he was come nigh to Bethphage and Bethany, at the mount called the mount of Olives, he sent two of his disciples,
>
> Saying, Go ye into the village over against you; in the which at your entering ye shall find a colt tied, whereon yet never man sat: loose him, and bring him hither.
>
> And if any man ask you, why do ye lose him? Thus shall ye say unto him, because the Lord hath need of him.
>
> Luke 19:28-31

Conclusion

Ministry is complicated! Life is complicated! It is not easy to follow a God whom you cannot see. It is not easy to follow a God whom you cannot hear.

If you have read this book, you would have encountered many wonderful keys that will make you fulfil your ministry in spite of the mysteries surrounding your service to God. It is important that you follow all the guidance that is coming from the Lord to you in this book. The mysteries in this book are leading you on the path to making full proof of your ministry.

One day you will say those words, "I have run my race and fulfilled my ministry!" May you receive the grace and power to make full proof of your ministry!

[illegible]

[illegible] the time was some [illegible]

[illegible]

[illegible]

Comments

[illegible]

[illegible]